WILD STYLE

Produced by Robert Hofler
A Fireside Book

Published by Simon & Schuster, Inc.
New York

BY ROBERT HOFLER
AND CYN. ZARCO
PHOTOGRAPHS BY
DOUG VANN

ILLUSTRATIONS BY
JAMES CHERRY

ACKNOWLEDGMENTS

Doug Vann thanks Ken Hansen photographic company for the Leica equipment, Jose at Professional Photo Supply for film and paper, and John Lei for advice and use of his studio.

Cyn. Zarco thanks Romeo, Adriana, Yuséff, Lara, Steve, Naveda, Michael, and the rest of the gang at Girl Loves Boy; Pat, Joey, Debbie, Andrê, Molly, and Mitchell at Patricia Field; Susan, Dana, Tom, Eugenia, Bayard, Pam, Patty, Margaret, and Michael at Modern Girls; Andy, Patsy, Jane, and Nick at Diane B.; Carmen and Pilar at Batislavia; and Joe Dolce for taking the time at Area. Also, Larry Jordan, Bruce Ricker, and Tony Gardner for good advice. And to Rose, Lorraine, Ed, and Mark for being there.

Robert Hofler thanks John Dombrowski at United, Mark Jacobson for advice on fashion, Robert Sabat for copy-editing expertise, Larry Sutter, and the more than 200 people who, in the fall of 1984, let us photograph and interview them for this book.

Special thanks to our editor, Charles Rue Woods.

CONTENTS

The seventies. The "Me Decade." The "natural look" was in, and everyone tried to look like Cheryl Tiegs. Such mediocrity in style deserved to end with a vengeance. The fashion scene was ready for a jolt, and when the punks took to the streets in the late seventies, they created a look so radically different and unlike anything seen before that "new" was an understatement.

Since then we've seen punk, radical punk, alternative punk, and new wave. However you classify it, the basic concept is the same. Originality of style has replaced the old, worn-out criteria for beauty. Symmetry is out and asymmetry is in, and nature has lost out to day-glo hair colors, outrageous makeup, and anything else that makes a human being look unlike the way humans were *supposed* to look a few years ago.

Wild style is based on these contradictions. It takes the identifiable and makes it abstract, throwing the perfect face off-balance, combining the toughness of leather with the elegance of lace, and creating the look of the future from fashions of the past. What were once considered facial flaws are now accentuated to make one look original, outrageous, and, in a different way, beautiful.

Punk started in the streets, and the spirit still lives there. In New York City *the streets* are below Fourteenth Street, and there is no place like it in the world. Call it "downtown"—or, if you have to be specific, the East Village, West Village, Soho, Noho, and Tribeca. This is where style is created, long before the press has time to label it.

In the East Village, Enz's is at one end of St. Mark's Place and the Pit is at the other. These two shops sell spikes, studs, and leather accessories for the tough post-punk look. Biss Quick is wearing rosaries and Sasha's got egg whites in her hair—all of which doesn't matter, as long as they wear black.

The British influences of estranged youth can still be felt, but here the alienated have been assimilated. Bondage pants don't mean bondage, and neon-red hair doesn't mean rebellion; it's just wild style.

Head farther east on St. Mark's Place and leave your dark garb behind. Here, the East Village still carries an occasional reminder of the hippies, who made this part of town their home. The loose, colorful clothes they wore have attracted the attention of today's designers, many of whom are young enough *not* to remember the sixties very well. Eva Goodman is one of these designers. She has designed a ping-pong ball dress she wants Gloria Gabe to sell in her shop, which is called 109 St. Mark's Place. Gloria says the dress is "unwearable," but that doesn't matter. She likes it anyway. Besides, around the corner and past Tompkins Square Park, Gracie Mansion is showing "foot fetish"

shoes in her art gallery that you can't wear either. Are they fashion or art or both? If both, so much the better. What's important is that designers and artists have the freedom to be witty yet serious about their work.

Backtrack west and leave the East Village behind. On Astor Place, Robert and Deb O'Nair are buying up sixties retro right off the street. There's great style in these old clothes, but the real challenge lies in giving them an eighties twist. Robert and Deb recommend Astor Place for street finds, but they have long hair and don't care much for the short precision cuts that everyone's crowding the door for at Astor Place Hair Cutters.

Hair used to be long or short, curly or straight, but today hair need never take the shape of hair. With names for haircuts like the "umbrella cut," "shelf cut," "spiral cut," and "crisscross cut," hair takes on a whole new dimension. A word of caution: Avoid Astor Place Hair Cutters on Saturdays. The crowds are awesome.

The same goes for Broadway, around the corner—unless, of course, you like to spend the day shopping, as thousands do. The promenade of lower Broadway divides the East Village from the West (Greenwich) Village, and on weekends there are more teen-agers here than in ten suburban shopping malls. Vintage village is fashion of the future taken from the past, and Antique Boutique carries the styles that are making a second coming. Here, wild style is knowing how to combine fashion elements—paisleys and plaids, rhinestones with military berets, fifties sweaters over shoulder pads.

"We don't repeat the exact look," says Patricia Field, who owns a boutique bearing her name on Eighth Street. "Everything that's gone down in the last twenty years has been added to the stew." Her customers are in love with bright colors, shiny fabrics, and playfully innovative designs that are the fashion signatures of the day. A girl holds up a metallic headdress: "Whadyacallit?" Patricia Field doesn't. "That's what I'm trying to put together here. Real designer clothing, like you would go into Bergdorf's or Bendel's for."

Soho, south of here, includes stores like Comme des Garçons, Diane B., and Artwear. Expensive chic, but chic nonetheless. If it's not an art gallery, it's a boutique. Or a hair salon. If you get to Thompson Street before three in the afternoon, Lara at Girl Loves Boy just might have enough time to put extensions in your hair to give you the "big hair" look for your night out at Area. Located in Tribeca, an exclusive artists' district south of Soho, Area is to fashion what Studio 54 was to disco in the seventies. You can dance, but you go to this club to be seen. Regardless of your wild style, here you have the area to breathe.

7

BLACK NO

Jobbi: "I'm not hard-core."

ART

he words NO POT SMOKING are stenciled on the old brownstone's front steps. Hippies used to crash here way back when. Later came the punks, then the new wavers. The next wave is already happening, though no one in the East Village, including these six people leaning against a wall, is sure what to label it. They'd just as soon not label it. Leave that to the uptown Manhattanites who come downtown on weekends to stare and snap photos of the "freaks" along St. Mark's Place.

A few yards down is the Pit, a biker's accessories shop that specializes in the hard-core black leather and metal gear these six are wearing.

"I'm not hard-core," says Jobbi, who is all in black except for her fluorescent red hair and makeup. For jewelry she wears chains, handcuffs, and metal studs. "Hard-core's a sloppier, rougher look," she goes on to say, unable—or unwilling—to classify her own

Gerold (right) wears a plaid "bum flap," while Robert (left) contemplates his German.

Gerold has tried many ingredients to keep his hair standing straight up. "The secret is Extra Super Hold Aqua Net," he says.

look. "But I used to have black hair. Too many people have that now." She isn't sure about any future experiments in style. "I'm trying to decide."

A shopkeeper on St. Mark's has the sides of his head shaved down to the nubs. He's asked what the new haircut is called. "It doesn't have a name, and it isn't new," he explains politely. He's been asked this question before. "I've had this haircut for over two years now."

"All fashion comes from the street," says an East Village makeup artist. In this part of New York City, a dozen haircutters and gallery owners and fashion designers will say the same thing. The environs of St. Mark's have so many boutiques, hair salons, vintage clothing stores, and art galleries, one thinks that people here must *need* a first look at the

Valerie's "pale look": white makeup and black hair.

Biss Quick: The rosaries go well with black.

fashion parade passing by.

Marlene looks, too. She is entranced by all the black leather and chains and studs and spikes underneath the Arnold Schwarzenegger poster. With her teased hair, layers of pancake makeup, and dark eyes ringed with Maybelline, Marlene has her own fashion statement to make. Polyester, even black polyester, however, is never going to make it on St. Mark's.

"Halloween! Halloween!" exclaims this former-cocktail-waitress type. Marlene, obviously, is from uptown.

The six against the wall don't respond. Not overtly, anyway. They don't like this woman. The only thing they hate more than hearing "Halloween! Halloween!" is "Cyndi Lauper! Cyndi Lauper!"

Gerold has had enough. He's already late for a rehearsal of an off-off Broadway play. It's called *The Onyx Fool,* and will premiere in a few week at a club in the area called 8 BC. In the play, Gerold gets to keep his hair riding high in a platinum-blond Mohawk. During the day, he isn't so lucky.

"I put my hair down and wear conservative clothes," he says regretfully, talking about his job at a charter bus line service in midtown Manhattan. "I slick the hair back with Tenax and shove it all over to the left. It looks like a normal conservative haircut. Even so, people will say, 'Oh, Andy Warhol!', 'cause it is so white."

Gerold has tried many different ingredients to keep his hair standing straight up, but nothing works like one particular brand of hair spray. "The secret is Extra Super Hold Aqua Net," he says,

giggling, almost embarrassed that he doesn't use something more exotic, or perhaps macho, like egg whites or gelatin. "It's the all-weather hair spray. I have five cans of it at home. You can't buy it in the city, so I have a friend get it for me in New Jersey. Only problem is, if I go out seven times a week, the can is gone."

Back on St. Mark's, two old men pass by Gerold's friend Robert. The two confer with each other, then tap the back of Robert's faded jean jacket. They do so with trepidation. "Excuse me, young man, but you've got it wrong." There's a trace of German in the old man's voice."It's not *'Ich hasse Leuten.'* The word is *'Leute,'* not *'Leuten.' "*

Robert thanks the man, then quickly has the errant *n* erased from his jacket. The German is now correct. It reads: "I hate people."

11

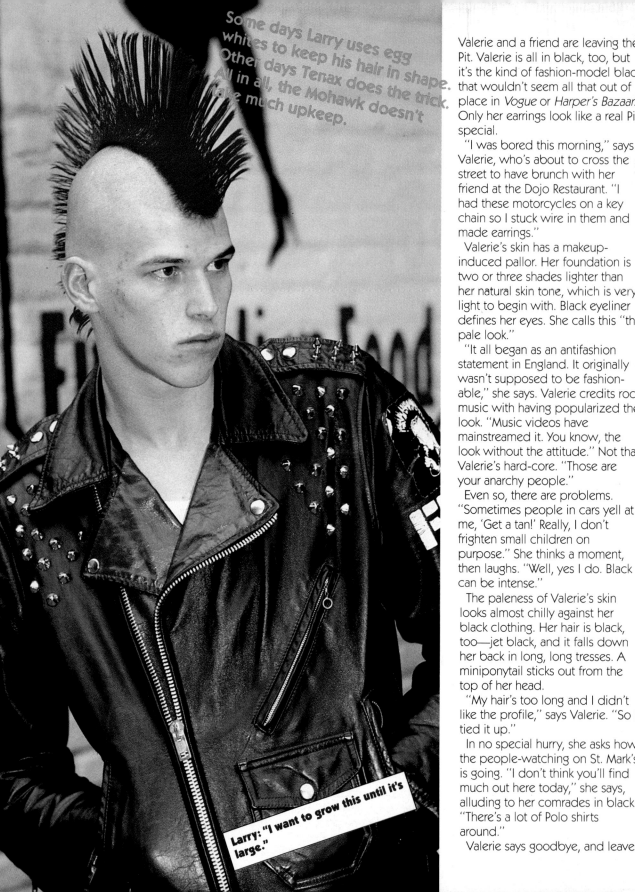

Some days Larry uses egg whites to keep his hair in shape. Other days Tenax does the trick. All in all, the Mohawk doesn't take much upkeep.

Larry: "I want to grow this until it's large."

Valerie and a friend are leaving the Pit. Valerie is all in black, too, but it's the kind of fashion-model black that wouldn't seem all that out of place in *Vogue* or *Harper's Bazaar.* Only her earrings look like a real Pit special.

"I was bored this morning," says Valerie, who's about to cross the street to have brunch with her friend at the Dojo Restaurant. "I had these motorcycles on a key chain so I stuck wire in them and made earrings."

Valerie's skin has a makeup-induced pallor. Her foundation is two or three shades lighter than her natural skin tone, which is very light to begin with. Black eyeliner defines her eyes. She calls this "the pale look."

"It all began as an antifashion statement in England. It originally wasn't supposed to be fashion-able," she says. Valerie credits rock music with having popularized the look. "Music videos have mainstreamed it. You know, the look without the attitude." Not that Valerie's hard-core. "Those are your anarchy people."

Even so, there are problems. "Sometimes people in cars yell at me, 'Get a tan!' Really, I don't frighten small children on purpose." She thinks a moment, then laughs. "Well, yes I do. Black can be intense."

The paleness of Valerie's skin looks almost chilly against her black clothing. Her hair is black, too—jet black, and it falls down her back in long, long tresses. A miniponytail sticks out from the top of her head.

"My hair's too long and I didn't like the profile," says Valerie. "So I tied it up."

In no special hurry, she asks how the people-watching on St. Mark's is going. "I don't think you'll find much out here today," she says, alluding to her comrades in black. "There's a lot of Polo shirts around."

Valerie says goodbye, and leaves

Bondage pants on St. Mark's Place: It comes down to style.

to cross the street with her friend. He's the one in the Lacoste jacket.

The first thing you notice about Larry is his Mohawk. A block away, people on St. Mark's are turning their heads to get a better look. "I want to grow this until it's large," says Larry. He shakes the bright strip of hair that splits his nearly bare skull in half. But it *is* large! Larry disagrees. "This is just medium. I want it to be immense."

Larry shaves his head himself. He uses Crazy Color to turn the hair bright pink. Some days he uses egg whites to keep it in shape; other days Tenax, a setting gel, does the trick. All in all, the Mohawk doesn't take much upkeep. "Sometimes I just leave it down," says Larry, who is often too busy studying cognitive science at Brown University to bother with his hair. "I let the sides grow out for a few days."

Then there are Larry's black bondage pants; they're the second thing you notice about him. The pants have strips of canvas that tie one leg to the other. He can walk, but not run, in them. Larry says they don't *mean* anything. "It just comes down to style. I heard a pretentious guy in Britain say, 'We live in a free country, but we might as well live in chains. That's why I wear bondage pants.' Well, I think that's a lot of bullshit."

Larry wants to know where he can buy some individual studs for his black leather jacket. He couldn't find any at Enz's, a British-import store on St. Mark's that carries black rubber skirts and bullet belts and ear spikes (like an ear stud, only sharper). Someone on the street suggests he go to the Pit, a few doors down.

Larry is one of the only people on St. Mark's who actually uses the word "punk." But then, he's from California.

"On the East Coast people have made a distinction between punk and hard-core," he says. "In L.A., hard-core simply refers to the degree of punk the person is. I'd call myself 'hard-core punk.'"

Paul Boles stands in the doorway of the Valencia Hotel. His girlfriend, who wears a white

Paul: "Some people won't wear a shirt unless it's black."

The bullet belt is a street find.

jacket and pink slacks that wouldn't turn a head at your local shopping mall, steps aside to check out the pizza at a corner stand.

Even on St. Mark's, Paul is intense. He's got on a ripped and sleeveless plaid shirt, a belt made out of bullet shells ("I bought it on the street for six bucks from a friend who needed money"), and an orange Mohawk ("it's Crazy Color") with black hair on the sides that he's let grow out. Like a lot of downtown people, he doesn't call his look *punk* or *new wave.* " 'Hard-core' is the word I hear a lot," he says.

Paul's hair has known many transitions. "First, it was platinum—really, really white," he begins, remembering back not too far. "And then it got too dark, so I dyed it red, which was just

obnoxious. Then I dyed it all black except for the top, which I left red. It's orange now because it's a semipermanent dye. It's faded to this color."

Unfortunately, Paul has to put up with the usual hassles connected with being more than just beautiful. "I'm not allowed into some restaurants. You know, the general aggravations. People resent you for it. At Disney World I wore a hat. I was afraid I'd draw more attention than Mickey Mouse. But people still saw a little orange." He laughs, not taking it at all seriously. "They ask me if it's my own hair. I hate that the most." He speaks without resentment, but is real thankful for a job at Commander Salamander, a new-wave boutique in Washington, D.C., that allows him the luxury of not having to lead a "double life."

Paul isn't philosophical about the black clothing. "We've adapted to it, latched onto it, made it ours. I know some people who won't wear a shirt unless it's black."

What will replace black hard-core as the next new look? "All fashion is retroactive," says Paul. "It all comes back eventually. I think long hair is the next thing. Boy George and the gender benders in England are a prelude to long hair."

Sasha's white Mohawk has a deco flair about it. Two small green wings frame that single, taller strand of magnificent white hair, giving it a symmetrical balance that's architectural, if not monumental. In front, strands of hair rush off her forehead. To call them bangs is an understatement. They're more like a landing pad for

Sasha on her haircut: "I don't pay for it."

"How do I get my hair to stick up like this?" says Sasha. "Egg whites. And I cut my own hair. I dye it, too, with Crazy Color."

supposed to keep people from hanging out on a private stoop. She turns this way, and then that. She even smiles a little. "Egg whites," Sasha responds before being asked. "I'm always asked that. How do I get my hair to stick up like this? Egg whites. And I cut my own hair. I dye it, too, with Crazy Color."

"I dyed your hair!" the girlfriend begs to differ.

"Yeah, well, sometimes!" Sasha snaps back. "At least I cut my own hair. I don't pay for it." On St. Mark's this is a point of intense pride. Whether you're creative enough to do your own, or just trendy enough to tell someone else what to do—it makes all the difference.

Even Sasha's hair has its good days and its great days. This is one of *those* days.

A couple of guys in black leather and metal studs rush by. "Hey, Sasha, your Mohican is really up there today!" they call out, not stopping on their way down the street. "Never seen it better!"

Sasha gives them a half-smile.

Joi cuts her own hair. She does Andrea's, too. At the moment Andrea is searching for used clothing downstairs at Trash and Vaudeville, an antique-clothing store. A curly-haired girl in a faded jean jacket and purple lipstick goes down to get Andrea. The three of them have been making the rounds of stores.

"No, I don't cut hair profes-sionally," says Joi in a very soft voice. "I'm a former market researcher." Joi's hair stands feathery on top while the sides are cropped very short in a ragged cut. Unlike many others here who dye their hair black, Joi doesn't heighten the contrast between hair and skin with white makeup. Her lips, in fact, are blood-red.

"My natural color is brown, and I didn't care for it," Joi explains. "My mother's hair is black, which I liked.

the aforementioned green-and-white headpiece.

Sasha is one-of-a-kind—even on St. Mark's—and she gets lots of requests to be photographed.

"How much?" she wants to know, not wasting a moment. "I'm in a hurry, here. Gotta run. And it took me all morning to get this hair together."

Her two friends try to up the price. "Ask for $25," says a girl. "Fifty dollars!" demands a guy, who points to Sasha's feet. "Wow! Shoot them, too! Heavy black boots!" he cries, mocking the gawking passersby.

Sasha accepts a five-dollar bill, then poses for about three minutes in front of an iron fence that's

Besides her hair, Joi's loose-knit sweater, stockings, and boots are also black. One of those boots is ringed around the ankle with several metal spikes.

"So what's going on?" asks Andrea, back up on the street, her body lost in an oversized vintage coat. Hair and coat are color-coordinated. Like Joi, she wears earrings made of black leather strips that are dotted with metal studs.

The curly-haired girl watches Joi. "She's so beautiful. I love her look."

Joi designed Andrea's hair, which is teased up and bleached on top with a long strand of hair that hangs down, cutting her face in

half. The Cubists would have approved. "I use soap in it," says Andrea. So does Joi in her feathery do. The women dampen their hair and rub a bar of soap through it—Ivory soap, good and cheap. The soap should not be lathered or it will leave the hair white and streaked when it dries. The hair is combed into the desired shape while still damp. When dried in the hair, the soap acts as a very, very strong fixative.

"Hair spray just doesn't work at all," says Andrea.

"No, it doesn't," says Joi.

Cindy Allen never wears anything but black to work. Her shop, which she co-owns with Karen Schachter, is a block up from St. Mark's on Ninth Street and Second Avenue. They call it Black Market. And so it is.

Inside, the dark gray walls look almost bright in contrast to the one-of-a-kind black dresses, the black felt hats, the black thermal underwear, the black bat jewelry, the black leather teddy bears, the black drinking straws, the black napkins. Everything black, black, black. Even the mirrored wall in

the back of this womb of a shop does not expand the space so much as embrace it.

"Personally, we're not immersed in black," says Karen—who, like Cindy, wears nothing but black. Professionally, it's another story. Karen and Cindy are about as immersed in this popular noncolor as one can get. Their delicate voices almost seem to disappear in the dark surroundings, as if blackness absorbs soundwaves as well as light.

Stepping out onto the sidewalk for just a moment, Cindy is wearing a stetson, a black leather miniskirt, and a one-of-a-kind black jacket by Prudence Moriarty, a favorite Black Market designer. Karen's black vest is also by Moriarty.

The store's name may have sinister overtones, but whereas the Pit is black hard-core, Black Market is black-noir chic with a very practical, feminine, and not at all criminal bent.

"Everyone looks well in black," says Karen, her face deliberately sans makeup, which she doesn't care to wear *ever*. "Black clothes don't get so dirty. It's comfortable. It stays in the background of what

you want to project."

For Cindy, that means makeup. "I like colors," she says, alluding to the bright makeup she has not put on her face this sunny afternoon. "I have a few colorful articles of clothing in my closet at home," she admits. "But I prefer black. Black will always be popular. I can't imagine it not."

Anne polishes her nails out in front of Astor Place Hair Cutters, just a couple of blocks west of St. Mark's. It's Saturday afternoon and there are dozens of other people out on the street with Anne, waiting to get their hair cut at the very popular barbershop. Anne paints all of her nails blue, except one. It gets treated to pink. The colors add a nice touch to the black-lace fingerless glove and the many chains and studded wristbands that occupy the rest of her left hand and arm. Black rubber bracelets ring the other arm. Polishing nails seems as good a way as any to pass the time.

One long braid of blond hair falls out of Anne's military beret. Will they be cutting it off inside? "No!" responds Anne, alarmed at such a

Joi, with soap in her hair: "Hair spray doesn't work."

Anne: "I'll wear anything."

H. KLIEGERMA
REAL EST
475

She dampens her hair and rubs a bar of Ivory soap through it. The soap should not be lathered or it will leave the hair white when it dries.

Lace and leather, chains and rubber, and a touch of pink.

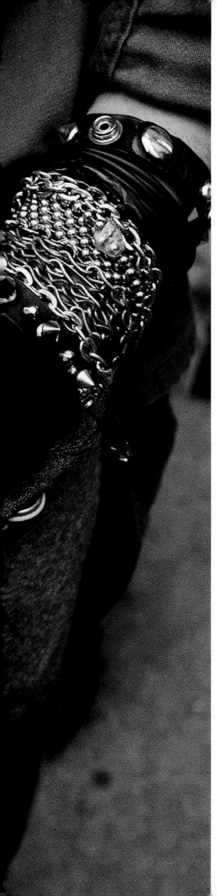

question. What kind of haircut is she getting at Astor Place? "No haircut!" Is she waiting for a friend who's getting a haircut? "No!"

Even with the crowd outside Astor Place Hair Cutters, Anne's unusual wrist-and-hand apparel is beginning to attract attention. "Why the leather and lace?" someone asks. "Why not?" asks Anne. "I'll wear anything."

Mary Jo's in black. She's at Pyramid Lounge, a club off Tompkins Square Park in the East Village. It's two blocks down from St. Mark's on Avenue A. This part of town used to be known as Alphabet City—before, as East Villagers will tell you, gentrification and all the boutiques and art galleries made the neighborhood chic.

There's no sign above the door at Pyramid, just a small black triangle. Inside, they play the latest dance music and there are little baby skeletons and bats and spiderwebs painted on the walls. Likewise, there's a small spiderweb tattooed on Mary Jo's right shoulder.

"At home I have this web made out of black leather and lace,".says Mary Jo, explaining the source of her inspiration. "I collect stuff off the street and put it in. I call it 'the web of life.' I'm going to keep adding stuff onto the one on my arm, too," she says. Right now her tattoo has only one small spider.

Unlike his friend Mary Jo, Steve hasn't dyed his hair black. He's left it blond, which isn't to say he never touches it. "I put anything in it I can get my hands on," says Steve. He takes a sip of his White Russian. "Soap, spray, egg whites . . ." The list goes on. Tonight his hair would be shoulder-length if only it weren't standing straight up. "Oh, it used to be longer," he says. "One day I was riding this motorcycle. My brother was driving, and the wind was just blowing my hair back and I was hacking at it with this razor. It was something."

A young man pops his head outside the door of Pyramid. He's looking for some people. When he doesn't find them, he climbs on top of the bar inside for a better look around. Still not spotting them, he begins to dance on the bar. Long necklaces twirl around his tall, thin body—but these are not long necklaces.

"My mother was going to be a nun," Israel explains, commenting on the many rosaries he wears. "I've had these rosaries since I was a small child. They were over my bed at home. I just tore off the cross on one of them and made it into an earring." He taps his left earlobe, and the silver body of Jesus swings back and forth for a moment.

Israel is right. In the dark light of Pyramid, the cross from his mother's rosary makes a great earring.

Many of the clothes and accessories photographed in this chapter can be bought in stores on St. Mark's Place. Enz's carries black rubber bracelets, six for $3; and black-lace fingerless gloves are $10 a pair. Bullet belts sell for $30; bondage pants for $55. Studded leather strip earrings are $6 apiece at the Pit, which also sells studded bootstraps for $12 and studded leather wristbands at prices from $6 to $12. Rosaries may be bought at your local R. C. gift shop.

Mary Jo and Steve at Pyramid.

"We called her 'the bride,'" says Claudia Renfro, describing her white tulle creation. "But it's not for weddings. The dress is black." Claudia hand-painted graffiti animals and abstract shapes on the dress, which is actually a very long black T-shirt. The hat she got on the street. "It's just a straw hat," says Claudia. "I cut off the top, turned it upside down, and spray-painted it black, then wrapped it in white tulle. I hate to give away all my secrets like this."

As with her very exotic hat, Claudia's designing career began on the street. "I was painting on scarves and T-shirts and selling them on Soho streets. I got a really good reaction." It was there that Claudia met a manufacturer of T-shirts and sweaters who bought a number of her hand-painted items. "It's hard to get a start," she says, "but you meet good people on the street."

(Dress, $100; hat, $30.)

During the day, it looks like any other building on East Eighth Street between avenues B and C. These tenements are all vacant, burnt-out, or.leveled to many tons of warlike rubble. Old men and young punks are occasional visitors; often they are the only occupants as they stare out from broken panes of glass at the deserted street below. It's not an easygoing part of town. Even the clubs and bars farther west, in relatively safe territory, have names like "Downtown Beirut."

At night, surprisingly, there are a few more traces of civilization on East Eighth Street. Cabs, and even the rare limo, are seen cruising by.

Designer Alexander von Benz is two women, Rebecca Alexander and Beth von Benz. "It's kind of a mystery," says Rebecca, talking about their assumed name. "It sounds like a count. Which is kind of like our clothes." Alexander von Benz's clothes are geared toward the classics, but with a modern twist. The pillbox hat is an example. Covered in a silver lamé brocade, it is pinned on the side with a heavy rhinestone brooch and dangling pearls. "The silver lamé is the twist here," says Rebecca. "Pillboxes have generally been done in more conservative fabrics, like velvet. Our accessories make the clothes look flashy." For Rebecca and Beth, hats and gloves and purses aren't just additions to the ensemble. "Without them," says Rebecca, "you just aren't dressed." (Hat, $60.)

BRIGHTER DAZE

Almost always they're looking for a club called 8 BC. Like Pyramid across nearby Tompkins Square Park, 8 BC is so discreet it has no use for a sign, and so the cabs have to look for clues in order to find it.

Tonight there are a lot of clues on the street. As a matter of fact, very well-dressed clues.

"Fashion designers are the rock stars of the eighties," says a young designer. There's a fashion show at 8 BC tonight, and the young designer, like a lot of others, is waiting to get inside. To some his point about rock stars and designers may be stretched so far it blurs, but this is, after all, the East Village—where fashion shows are the fastest way for a club owner to fill the place up.

"It's like going to a rock concert," says Gloria Gabe. This is Gloria's fashion show. She's not a designer, but it's her shop, 109 St. Mark's Place, that is featuring the work of seventeen of its designers.

The fashion show begins with a feminist performance by Angela Pringle. The actress clutches her bare breasts while two men undulate around her and a recorded voice details their sexist exploits. The crowd at 8 BC pretty much ignores the half-naked woman. They want to watch people with clothes on, after all—bright, colorful, and very, very different clothes.

Angela used to model for Gloria. Most of the models in the 109 St. Mark's Place fashion show are "just friends" of the designers. Many double as makeup artists and hairstylists, and it's not unusual for one designer to model another's fashions. There's a feel, not only of community, but of family, and sure enough, Gloria's husband Steven, who co-owns 109 St. Mark's Place, is in charge of music and sound.

Tonight a jazzed-up version of Puccini's "Un bel dì" moves the oversized plaids across the stage. Lifesaver pants dance to sixties

"I call it my conservative punk," says Maira Gomez. Her orange-plaid jumpsuit is big and roomy, with extra-large pockets on the sides. Like a lot of Maira's creations, it is not a specific size and can be worn with or without a belt to create a variety of looks. "If you stick your hair up and put on some wild makeup, as the model does here, it's punk," says Maira. "But without that, it's a more conservative look. I wouldn't, however, wear it to a job interview." (Jumpsuit, $90.)

"A friend of mine found this picture frame and silk screen in the garbage." Eva Goodman is explaining how this particular pair of bright yellow pants came into being. "He wanted the frame and was going to throw away the 'Lifesaver' silk screen and I said, 'No, it's great! We've got to do something with it.'" And so the pants were born. Very baggy, they are cinched with d-rings and supported with suspenders. They fit any sex and any size. "If you're tall, the pants are short," says Eva. "And if you're short, they're not."

Eva creates many of her clothes from found objects. The spiral-pattern shirt is made from old fabric. The vest is trimmed with the same day-glo ribbons used to mark runways at airports. "I see something and it inspires me. I take it beyond what it is."

(Pants, $80; shirt, $50; vest, $60.)

bubblegum music, and the tribal chants of Philip Glass inspire the brocades—and vice versa. Vivaldi accompanies a particularly extravagant hand-painted outfit by Claudia Renfro. The music may be sedate, but there's nothing reserved about the audience's reaction.

"Clubs like 8 BC are very liberating," Gloria is saying as the crowd shouts its approval. "People in the East Village wear clothes at clubs or for performances in bands. They can experiment with fashion. In these environments, you don't fear wearing crazy designs or colors."

If all art must have its theme, Gloria's is youth. 109 St. Mark's Place showcases fashion by the youngest, most innovative designers in the city. "Right now, a store like mine could only happen in New York City," Gloria insists. "Young designers here wait on tables or work in clubs. Other cities, like Milan, where I'm from, are too provincial for that. But here, it's okay to wait on tables until you get a start. Young designers—they're like actors, always waiting on tables."

Besides the clubs, art galleries are the other big influence on East Village designers. Gloria Gabe talks with enthusiasm about an art piece at the Gracie Mansion gallery, around the block from her shop. "Take the Liz and Dick Bedroom (there it's formally entitled The City That Never Sleeps, by Rhonda Zwillinger.) You can buy shoes that go with the bedroom, but you can't wear the shoes. At my shop I have clothes that aren't wearable, too." The concept of clothes as art objects excites Gloria. "They're experimental like a dress with ping-pong balls attached that Eva Goodman designed. She did another that was shaped like the Guggenheim Museum."

More practical, wearable clothes also share a strong crossover influence. In fact, the designer and artist are often one. "Some artists may have a painting at Gracie Mansion and a painted T-shirt at my shop."

Sur Rodney (Sur) and Gracie Mansion, co-directors of the Gracie Mansion art gallery, relax for a moment in the "Liz and Dick Bedroom" unwearable shoes from the lower left corner are from the "Foot Fetish" series, also by Zwillinger.

BLADE RUNNER

BARBER
STYLIST

ASTOR PLACE
HAIR CUTTERS

S

A

ten-year-old boy walks into Astor Place Hair Cutters. Just off Broadway, the barbershop is at the crossroads of both the East and West Village and a lot of what's happening in hair today. The boy is with his mom. She's in a pantsuit; he's sporting black denims. Very St. Mark's. The kid wants a "spike cut," a hairstyle that is achieved by shaving the sides of the head very close and cutting the hair on top at radically different lengths, so that it stands up spiky.

Mom isn't sure. "His grandmother won't understand," Mom tells Enrico Vezza, co-owner of Astor Place. Mom is worried. Son is adamant. Any other barbershop owner would tell his potential customers to take their spikes elsewhere and fight it out. But this is Enrico Vezza—the Barnum & Bailey of hair, the Eternal Earth Father of barbers everywhere. Here is a man who has a solution for every solution.

"Tell you what," says Enrico in a calm, paternal voice. He takes a white stick of Butch Wax off a dusty, overcrowded shelf. "Let the

ASYMMETRICAL CUT

boy have his 'spike cut,' and every time he goes to see Grandma, just put an ounce of Butch Wax on. It'll keep the hair flat and Grandma won't know a thing." Mom is relieved and Enrico's got another happy customer.

Three feet away, Giovanni, a haircutter, is getting mild complaints from a steady customer. "After two weeks my hair falls down on the sides," says the pretty blonde. "No problem," says Giovanni. Everything is *no problem* at Astor Place. The girl braces herself in the barber's chair. "Okay, let's go!" she says, waiting for Giovanni to shave the sides of her head right down to the scalp.

Enrico gives a broad smile. "Love these new haircuts. Every two weeks and these kids gotta get another one. Love 'em!"

Later, Giovanni confesses that some haircuts aren't exactly *no problem*. "Shaving a person's name into sides of head," he admits in halting English, "is no easy trick."

Astor Place is an old-fashioned barbershop with old-fashioned

barbers. Few of these men are young. Many have graying hair—when they have hair at all—and they wear it hanging over their ears and the collars of their blue smocks. They are poor candidates for any fashion's vanguard, but in the world of wild style, where contradictions not only abound but somehow belong at the very heart of inspiration, Astor Place Hair Cutters is the home of the very short, very precise haircut.

A sign on the wall reads: "We speak Spanish, Italian, Russian, and a little English." Enrico wrote that one himself, and sure enough he's got a barber named Joseph from Mtsensk, U.S.S.R., who's been with him for three years.

Joseph, who emigrated here five years ago, thinks Astor Place is "gangbusters."

"Never make it twice the same job," he says. "Russia was nothing like this. Astor Place was nothing three years ago like this either," Joseph adds, referring to the current trend in wild and short haircuts. One of Joseph's proudest accomplishments is a spiral-and-shave cut he did for an artist/model, who gave him a drawing

SPIRAL CUT

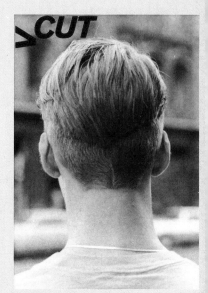

CUT

for his unusual hair design.

"It's all up to the person," Enrico is quick to explain. "We work it through with the customers, what they want. And if it works out, we name the cut after them."

Suzy Cut. Big Tony Cut. Tina Cut. But Enrico wants *everybody* looking good when they leave his establishment. He's free with advice. "If you've got small features, short hair is best. If you're a guy like me"—he puffs out his fleshy cheeks—"more hair is better."

He has little time for the sugar solutions and egg-white recipes that people now use to keep their hair standing straight and tall. "Butch Wax," says Enrico. "Good old-fashioned Butch Wax does the trick. Been around since the fifties." (This thick and heavy hair fixative is an Astor Place favorite. It retains its semisoft, somewhat moist consistency without drying and leaving the hair stiff, as Tenax can.)

Enrico relishes Astor Place's reputation for crazy cuts. He's the first to admit that most people come here looking for "normal, regular haircuts." But it's the more eccentric requests that stick in his mind, like the man who had an arrow shaved into the side of his head. "I asked the guy, 'Why an arrow?', and he said, 'So I know where I'm going.'" Enrico twirls a dead Corona through his fingers. "I love these kids. Love 'em!"

Enrico may be fifty, but nothing fazes this guy—not even the black hard-core look that's so popular only two blocks away on St. Mark's Place. "Some of these girls come in here wearing leather and studs and swastikas. They look like S & M prostitutes, y'know." Enrico's making a real ugly face, but all at once his blue eyes bounce. "And they're so sweet. So sweet! They do this as a kick. Love 'em!"

Astor Place is a din of noisy confusion. As the barbers' chairs fill, Enrico turns up the volume on his tape deck. Soon the Pointer Sisters are competing with a loudspeaker that calls out the names of the waiting customers, who overflow out of the small shop onto the street. At Astor Place reservations are neither required nor tolerated. On Saturdays—"when the tourists

CRISSCROSS CUT

31

TAIL CUT

come," says Enrico—there are easily a hundred on the curb outside waiting two hours for a precision cut.

"I tried using a bullhorn, but it didn't work," says Enrico, who's practically shouting now to make himself heard. "The batteries ran down. It wasn't loud enough, either." Which is understandable. He points to the microphone, which is operated by his sons, Paul and John. "I've had this loudspeaker and microphone for about a year. Just like Sinatra. Some kids come in here and go, 'Let me sing a song,' " sings Enrico. "Ah, it's just part of the hype, y'know."

Enrico laughs. This is a man who knows his business, and his business is a lot more than haircuts. "It has to be a fun place," he says. "What am I selling? *Haircuts!*" He holds out his hands as if for mercy. "We're not superpeople. We're high school dropouts. Well, not quite. It took me five years. But I made it."

LITTLE TONY CUT

names. "The 'Little Tony Cut' is named after Tony Curtis, the way he had his hair back in the fifties." How's that? "A spot perm in the front and very short every place else."

And the "Guido Cut," another Astor Place favorite? "Guido in Italian is like 'Hey, Charlie!'" That's a Guido—very short on the sides and long on top and in the back.

Clap. Clap. Clap. Another barber is ready to go. "I'm thinking about getting them whistles instead," says Enrico. "It'll add to the hype."

Two pretty teenage girls carry out Hefty bagfuls of shorn hair. Out in the alley, the bags pile up as the hair comes off inside. Despite the girls, Astor Place is a real mess. And there's little doubt that Enrico planned it that way. The mirrors are smoky and the pistachio-green walls are littered with hundreds of badly lit Polaroid shots of smiling customers. Each photo has its name attached.

Ah-Ha Cut. Rainbow Cut. Opening-Night Cut.

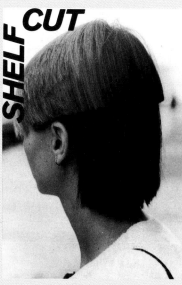

SHELF CUT

Clap. Clap. Clap. Every other minute, it seems, another barber's chair is empty. There are over a dozen men working clippers in this hole-in-the-wall joint. Clapping hands is their signal that they're ready for Enrico's sons to send another customer.

It wasn't always so at Astor Place. Even though the business has been in the Vezza family since the forties, Enrico almost closed his shop a few years ago. "The place was very shaky. All of a sudden, a couple of years ago, we started noticing guys asking for very fifties haircuts. Flattops. Crew cuts. Short hair suddenly looked so new!" recalls Enrico, who stopped "working the chair" back in 1964. "I went, 'Hey, hold on here! We've got something.'

"These names I give the haircuts . . ." Enrico pauses to lower his voice. "It's hype, y'know." Then suddenly, dead serious, he points a finger at his heart. "But you can't bluff a haircut. No way."

Enrico explains a few of the

HEDGE CUT

What-Is-This Cut.

Models who charge $100 an hour to be photographed sit for Enrico's Polaroid, then pay him $6 to $15—the going Astor Place haircut rate. Their head shots and Smirnoff ads are also up on the wall, usually signed: "Astor Place, the Best."

Enrico takes out a brobdingnagian bottle of Scotch. "Not till after five," he says, having second thoughts, and back goes the half-empty bottle among the clutter of oil containers, clippers, and hair blowers.

A red Mohawk with a girl walks in. She's looking to have her sides reshaved. "Butch Wax," says Enrico, revealing the secret of her hair's staying power. "Nothing but Butch Wax."

The Mohawk is just back from England. "Hey, Enrico, I think long hair is making a return in London!" she cries across the noisy, smoky, crowded room.

Enrico, for the first time that day, stops dead. "Oh, I hope not!"

A woman is trying on what they call "Marilyn earrings." As in Marilyn Monroe. She looks in the mirror at the dangling rhinestone earrings. Slowly her eyes drop to her gray turtleneck sweater. The woman just isn't sure. "I don't think I have the body for these earrings," she tells a clerk.

"Nobody has the body for these earrings anymore," says the clerk, her own figure covered in a madras jacket. "Don't let that stop you."

Antique Boutique is *the* department store for hip nostalgiacs who would rather live in the future through the past. On Broadway between the East and West Village, Antique Boutique is located in a part of town that has as many vintage clothing stores as a punk's ear has studs. Unlike many of those other stores, however, Antique Boutique is definitely not for vintage purists. Here you create your own wild style by taking the past and the present and mixing them up, together, and around. In a fast-food world where fashion is mass-produced, sometimes the only way to come up with a one-of-a-kind look is to look back with both your eyes wide open.

"Create your own style from the past," says Michael, echoing the credo of most Antique Boutique people. He describes the colorful diversity of his own one-of-a-kind outfit as "Hollywood–Coconut Grove extravagance with a little dash of today and 'Dallas' and tomorrow." Which is which doesn't really matter.

Michael is a "personal shopper" who buys clothes for many celebs who want to go vintage but don't have the time to look around for those rare finds. His gold ear cuff is a gift from Christo, the conceptual artist who goes around wrapping a lot more than just ears. Catherine Deneuve gave Michael his sea-foam-green antique shirt. "She said it looked good with my eyes," Michael recalls. "I said, 'Are

VINTAGE

Michael puts together a Hollywood—Coconut Grove outfit: a dash of today, "Dallas," and tomorrow.

you drunk?' " Michael picks out kimonos for Deneuve and gabardine shirts, too. "They're soft and so is she."

Michael also sports a deco rhinestone pin, and his checkered jacket and iridescent trousers are "fancy formal fun wear" from the fifties. And the string tie provides that touch of "Dallas."

Like a lot of people at Antique Boutique, Louise is into vintage, but she's no addict. "I wear only extravagant things," says Louise, who works in the store's boutique at Fiorucci, uptown. "I don't wear college sweaters from the fifties, you know." Her big attraction to vintage clothing is the fabrics and design. "If the fabric's already lasted thirty years, you know it's good. Designers come in and buy clothes. They copy the design and turn around and sell it for $600. Let's face it, people today are more attracted to Marilyn Monroe than the Thompson Twins."

Louise's black dress is a reproduction of a forties ballroom gown. "I paid too much for it," says Louise, who reveals the price to be around $300, "but it was my birthday." Part Marilyn, part punk, Louise dons a fifties rhinestone earring and four tiny red studs.

So how eclectic can you get? Out on the street with Louise, Albert puts together an early-sixties dinner jacket, black long underwear, and white wool socks. For a more casual look, he combines a fifties sweater with an Indian turban. Since the sweater was too large, Albert added shoulder pads, even though size wasn't the only consideration in his

Albert in tuxedo and Louise in ballroom gown: giving old clothes new shapes.

fashion decision.

"The pads are from a Norma Kamali jumpsuit," he says, pulling out the bright purple pads. "They give the sweater a new shape, which I think is very romantic."

This is what Albert calls "RDing," that is, "redesigning" antiques. It's his profession at Noamex, Antique Boutique's parent company and distributor. Besides his shoulder-pad trick, Albert suggests a number of other ways to update old fashions: Stitch old doilies to sweaters; wear black tights underneath dresses; fashion skirts from old lace tablecloths; and add leather collars to madras jackets from the sixties. Antique Boutique then sells these reconstructed jackets as tuxes.

These kinds of "make-over" antiques hold no interest for Alvin. He's the only true purist in the group. "I like fifties clothes," he says, talking about a decade he wasn't even around for. "They're very full. I don't mix styles or periods." Alvin creates his authentic mafioso look by mixing shades and textures—not decades.

Sometimes the past need only be hinted at to create your own personal wild style. An unusual pair of gloves. Some outrageous costume jewelry. "Accessorize and make it distinctive, one of a kind," recommends Susan. It's only a little lace and tulle, but crossing Broadway, Susan's cocktail hat from the forties stops more traffic than a blinking red light. Not an original, the hat is an "exaggeration" of an old design from the period. "During the World War II years, fabrics and cuts were simple. They had to be," says Susan. She takes a tip from the past. "Hats were the only way to individualize."

A fifties look. Some hats from the

forties. And a bold return to the sixties. When can one expect Antique Boutique to start stocking seventies stuff?

"Never!" insists Harvey Schefrin, co-owner with his brother Gary of Antique Boutique and Noamex. "You can't do much with polyester," he says, alluding to that "nerd decade."

Right now, sixties clothes, such as the madras jackets, are the most popular items in the store. According to Harvey, though, the sixties mod/preppy/hippie look is more a result of supply than demand. "I don't have as much thirties stuff, so I don't sell as much. Victoriana moves very, very fast. But collectors snap that up."

Harvey, who calls himself the "George Washington of antique clothing," started selling vintage wear back in 1958. "Mostly to Europe, where there was a hunger for Americana," he recalls. But the real fad in vintage began with students in the sixties. "It was a military put-down of the Vietnam War. We sold a lot of World War II stuff then—field jackets, pilot jackets."

If army khakis can make a comeback, then why not a nice pink leisure suit? Harvey repeats himself: "Never!"

Okay, but who's to say when the next wave passes by, that a "nerd look" isn't floating around out there somewhere? The future is an awfully big ocean.

Prices of vintage clothes at Antique Boutique vary radically depending upon condition, style, and supply of certain garments. Reproductions are more consistent in price. Gayle's red prom dress sells for $125. The forties lace-and-tulle hat, worn by Susan, is $145. And the Marilyn earrings range in price from $25 to $45.

Susan's lace-and-tulle cocktail hat: an "exaggeration" of a forties design.

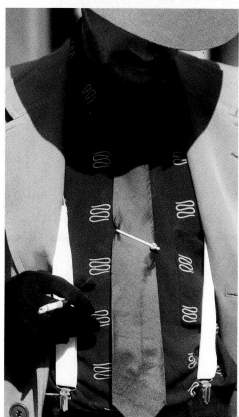

Alvin creates his mafioso look: "I don't mix styles or periods."

STREET

You can buy it in a store or you can buy it on the street. One thing is for sure—the street's cheaper.

Kimberly Seltzer's look reflects a Victoriana of the mind. Take away one element of her ensemble and the illusion is shattered. "I found the morning coat on the sidewalk on Third Street," says Kimberly. "I never even got it dry-cleaned. I paid fifty cents for the vest on Avenue A. And the pins are just gifts from friends. All reproductions, I'm afraid." Dippity-do keeps her hair slicked back and in place.

In addition to having a real

Kimberly in a morning coat she found on the sidewalk.

passion for Charles Dickens, Kimberly is a painter who specializes in missionary symbolism. "It's a cross between Italian classicism and comic books," she explains.

More vintage village on-a-budget can be found at the Canal Street Flea Market, on the corner of Greene and Canal. The prized possession here, though, isn't for sale.

Atop her stool, Beverly Chester looks down upon racks of antique clothing through sunglasses that would put a wing-tipped Cadillac to shame.

Beverly at the Canal Street Flea Market: The sunglasses aren't for sale.

"They're from the early fifties," says Beverly, who's been selling old clothes here for the past three years. "They were handmade in France. And, yes, they're not for sale."

Draped over Beverly's dress are three rayon paisley scarves, the kind that were popular during World War II. But what really attracts attention is Beverly's straw hat. "It's from around 1910," she says. "It was worn by women at picnics. This one came with three roses. I turned it into this monument to Mother—my mother and mothers everywhere. I also make treasures out of trash," says Beverly, pointing out the more colorful bracelets that wrap her wrists. "It's a recycling process. It's a healthy way to make a living. No one's getting hurt and I'm not polluting the air. That's important to me."

Deb O'Nair and Robert are also street smart. They just came from Astor Place, where they find a lot of sixties clothes for sale right out on the sidewalk. "Big wide belts, big heavy medallions, lots of paisley," says Robert. "It's what I'm after." Sometimes, when he can't find what he wants, Robert tailors his street finds into Nehru jackets and stovepipe pants, like the ones he's wearing today. Despite their apparel, both Deb and Robert reject the "mod" label.

"It's more of a sixties garage-punk thing," says Deb, who's in a band called the Fuzztones. "The look is derivative of those underground bands like the Seeds, Chocolate Watchband, and Music Machine— the beginning of psychedelic music." Even though she was only seven or eight at the time, Deb says she remembers a lot about that era.

"I had these white go-go boots, and I'd get together with my girlfriends and dance up on a chair. That's what I wanted to be when I grew up: a go-go girl."

This may explain Deb's long, blond hair, which is no Astor Place precision cut. "It's like Nancy Sinatra in a biker movie, a streetwise image. Seductive and sexy at the same time. And a little witchy, too."

The Seeds inspired Robert's pageboy haircut. "It's that Prince Valiant British-American garage-psychedelic thing," he says.

Come again?

"Well, let's just say it's not techno-psychedelic."

Whatever. If fashion pundits are to be believed, Deb and Robert's long hair is the shape of things to come back.

Some people don't have to go to the streets to find their clothes. Leslie found her day-glo minidress at home. "It's my mom's from the sixties," she says. The sixties themselves, however, don't ring any bells with Leslie, even though she's wearing the mini, go-go boots, psychedelic earrings, bright pink stockings, and a ponytail down to her waist. (It's a hair extension.) Actually, Leslie's at a loss about how to describe her own individual look. A friend on St. Mark's tries to help out.

"It's rock clubs, rock movies, glam rock, and rock music," he says. Leslie nods her approval. Her wardrobe, she feels, is pretty complete. "But I am looking for a pair of platform boots." When told that a guy at Patricia Field boutique has a great pair, Leslie says she knows him. "Yeah, I'd like to take Joey, knock him over, and spray those boots silver."

Debbie (right) watches Pat at play at the makeup counter. "I fly to Paris and London to shop for the best makeup. I carry everything by Biba . . . neon lipsticks, nail polish, and eye watercolors by Barry M., and Barbara Hulanicki . . . all from England. And from France, Bourjois—a line of translucent eye powders and blushes."

Ganzo Studio's Maria Minichiello: "A naked back is always attractive."

Patricia Field

"Look at those great boots!" Pat is pointing to a pair of furry, Afghanistan-looking ones on a woman who's just walked into the store that bears her name—Patricia Field. "Who's to say whether it's in or it's out? What's fashion anyway?" she shouts above the music. "Fashion is created by people who express their moods with what they wear. It's that simple." She pets her cat, Kitty Boy, then adds, "It's not, 'Do I wear a skirt or do I wear pants?', it's a mood or a feeling. And whatever I'm feeling at the moment I just let it out on the store." She smiles. "I'm lucky. I don't have to sell 20,000 witch shoes to pay the rent."

Patricia Field's boutique, on well-traveled Eighth Street in Greenwich Village, is unique on the New York fashion scene. Here, new American and British designers premiere their wares long before they show up on the racks in any other shop in town, months before the fashion mags can even give the latest fad a name. Pat talks about her designers. "I can't say I find them in rock clubs or at art galleries or fashion shows. We live in the young American design jungle. This is *my* environment. This is downtown New York! They're right here!"

Pat shouts out advice to her customers as they stand in front of the wall-sized mirror and try on different hats—Dalmatian fun-fur pillbox hats, blue panné velvet hats, Ave Maria leather berets. "You know what that would look

ESTATE OF THE ART

good with?" Then to Joey, who literally works the store, she says, "Where's that red crocheted hat with the long Chinese braid? You know the one . . ."

"These things are my medium," says Pat, making a sweeping gesture with her free hand to include the shoe racks in the rear of the store, the estate-of-the-art designer jewelry under glass, the surplus wear folded on the floor, and the huge makeup counter. "Artists paint with paints, other times they sculpt, and other times they make collages. These are my tools. Paint would be equivalent to designers, clay would be equivalent to surplus, and costumes would be like metal. I have to talk on these levels because when you talk on fashion

levels, it gets too boxed in. That's not really what we do here."

Joey walks over with an Andrê Walker "whale" coat, a light-blue, pink, and yellow checkered one that looks like a warm baby blanket. Trying it on as if he were Monroe and it were a fresh mink, Joey says, "This is definitely a car coat." Standing to the side, the designer, Andrê, observes this tender moment with a satisfied grin. Pat suddenly stands up, takes one look at Debbie in a pink leather ensemble and zebra tights, and says, "I bet this coat will look fabulous over that pink suit." Andrê likes it, and Debbie buries her hands in the pockets of the coat and practically purrs. She tries on another whale coat. This time it's red plaid and reversible, with a

cinched waist and winged shoulders. Debbie asks, "What do you call this coat, Andrê?"

"Gosh, I dunno," he says, looking puzzled and trying to remember. "What do I call this?" he asks himself. "The shortback whale coat, yeah . . ." He points to the outline of a whale stitched into the collar of the coat. "That was the whole theme," he says. The curved lines suggest whale fins. Why did he choose whales as the inspiration for his '84 winter line? Andrê answers in a child's voice, "I like them."

"You see, this is designer clothing," Pat continues. "I mean, it's not cheap stuff. Right, Andrê?" Andrê nods and repeats the retail price—$400. "So, the whole thing is that this age group, all they really

43

have had up to this point is funky wear, antique clothes, or street fashion," explains Pat. "That's what I'm trying to put together here. Real clothing, like you would go into Bergdorf's or Bendel's for."

Charles and Maria Minichiello, a brother-sister designer team known as Ganzo Studio, stop by to say hello. Maria is wearing one of her sexy red dresses with a plunging, deep V-neckline in the back. Mitchell, who's behind the counter, lets out a whistle. "This dress is subtle and in good taste, but very sexy," says Maria. "We show a lot of collarbone and backbone. No matter how big or small a woman is, a naked back is always attractive."

Chained to the rack on one side of the store is what's left of the

Stephen Sprouse/Stefano leather jacket collection—a portrait of Christ on the back of a silver jacket, one of Fidel Castro, another of Marilyn Monroe. "We bought the jackets initially," says Joey. He gives the history behind the collaboration. "Pat saw Stefano's work and she liked it, especially the Mona Lisas. So she commissioned him to do the jackets. They're pretty reasonable at $1,500, when you think that you're getting an original piece of artwork *and* a great jacket!"

Pat explains how she selects merchandise for the store and does her buying. "I don't plan anything. I go wherever I feel I will find clothes that will fit my mood. I'll go anywhere to find good things." Lately, Pat has been buying

a lot of clothing and accessories in London. "I carry mostly British and American designers because that's where I find things that are more expressive. Like Katherine Hamnett and World's End."

On one of her trips to England, Pat brought back an incredible pair of platform boots for Joey. He couldn't find any like them in New York City. It seems that the sixties is making a comeback. Pat might agree, but with qualifications. "Late-sixties clothes is one of the inspirations, one factor that people are responding to now," Pat says. "But it's not a look that's back again. Everything that's gone down in the last twenty years has been added to the stew. We draw from that time. We don't repeat the exact look." Pat isn't getting

specific. She doesn't like labels. "The design may be similar," she continues, "but the fabric is different. That kind of thing."

Pat is making a point. "That's the whole trick that everybody misses. It's not, 'Package it and put it in a Kellogg's box.' It's more creative than that. This store is a result of my own artistic expression. It's the other people who make fashion out of it."

Since Pat always seems to be on top of the next fashion craze, she's often asked, "What's next?"

"Cockroach fashion," she says, laughing, standing around the beaded headgear, the metallic boots, the hand-painted leather jackets. Of course, she's joking, although she says, "Antifashion would be very nice. It's all getting a little overdone."

Debbie and Joey on Eighth Street: Late-sixties clothing is one of the inspirations.

"Art and clothing have always been our theme," says Susan Balcunas, standing next to her best friend, Dana Fraser, outside their boutique, Modern Girls. It's Saturday and a crowd has gathered around Thompson and Houston streets to photograph the pair—one tall blonde, one tall brunette. They're wearing clothing they designed themselves. Dana is in a post-mod geometric black-and-white minidress over a white cotton turtleneck and black capris; Susan's dressed in a black-and-white unstructured reversible hound's-tooth jacket with orange lining over a herringbone maxi-jumper.

Modern Girls

"Just before we opened," Susan continues, "Dana did a show, and Max Black, the bartender at Raoul's . . . well . . . he's a poet and he used to title a lot of her paintings. And one of the paintings was of the two of us, and it was called *Modern Girls*." Susan gives Dana a funny look. "You should have seen the painting," she says. "It was kind of bizarre." They both giggle, and suddenly you realize that these girls are really just big teenagers. Susan goes on, "So that's what we decided to call the store—Modern Girls—like us."

Dana explains the arrangement. "I'm more interested in art and painting," she says. "Originally, Susan was going to do clothing, and I . . . well . . . it was going to be a gallery to show art, which it still is. We have art up on the walls,

and the rest of the store is fashion."

"I've been making clothes most of my life," Bayard says, pushing a lock of primary-red hair away from his face, "since the time I got suspended from junior high school for telling the principal to screw herself. My mother didn't know what to do with me, so she taught me how to sew." Bayard's wearing three of his creations—a kimono-style long red jacket over a blue-and-red tartan-plaid shirt and loose-fitting trousers.

Pam Meyer, a costume-jewelry designer, walks up wearing a light-blue cashmere overcoat from Bayard's 1983 fall collection. She has on the numbers 8 and 5 as earrings. Pam leans on a parked car to listen to Bayard. He clasps his hands together and continues, "See, I'm not really a designer. I'm

"I'm into snakes," says Patty Pomerantz at Modern Girls. She wears one coaster-size earring. "I made the rubber mixture myself. I mix paint in with it and pour it into flat molds."

a painter—that's really what I want. It's just that the clothing took off quicker, so that's what I'm doing. It pays for the painting."

Standing against the red door next to Modern Girls, designer Michael Wylde and an uncanny lookalike, Chryst Skleros, bring to mind an early Beatles poster of the fab four posing in a London mews—though this time there's only two of them. A scruffy lot, these blokes.

"I go back and forth to London," says Michael, wearing his favorite color, black. He's got on a long-sleeved frayed linen number over black leather pants, dark sunglasses, and rings of black rubber bracelets on his wrist. "I spent the summer there and it was fun, but I still think it's better here in New York. There's more of a fashion scene here."

A newcomer to Modern Girls, Michael only started designing clothes a year ago. His first fashion show was at Beulah Land, on East Tenth Street and Avenue A, where he moonlights as a bartender.

Michael (left) with Chryst: "I did some white things for summer as a sacrifice."

"The only things I do are black, like this." Michael points to his top. "I also do skirts, dresses, winter coats, and wraps. I did some white things for summer as a sacrifice, but when I brought them around to stores people went 'What is this? You didn't do this! It's *white*!' And I said, 'I know. I'm trying to diversify.'"

"The first thing I ever made was a red-suede miniskirt." Eugenia speaks breathily between puffs off a Dunhill. Her jet-black hair escapes from the top of her felt Foreign Legion cap, which she designed along with the rest of her outfit: a simple black-wool jersey blouse over a long straight skirt that has pleats down to her hips. "It was 1975 and I was living in Leningrad at the time, a place where fashion virtually doesn't exist. I wore it on the street, with my platform shoes and a black-and-white, polka-dot blouse with a low décolletage, and I was promptly arrested by the militia for 'looking like a Martian.'"

Dana and Susan laugh along with her as she tells them the rest of her amazing story. "Russian clothes are usually nondescript. But they're made from natural fibers, only

because Russia hasn't developed the machinery to make polyester yet." She pauses. "In the seventies the trendiest woman in Russia would be wearing a pair of Levi's that she bought on the black market for $300." From the tone of her voice, Eugenia probably never owned a pair of blue jeans, and still doesn't to this day. She explains how the Soviet black market works. "People usually buy clothes right off the backs of foreign tourists, whether it's fashionable or not, then sell them on the black market for ridiculous prices.

"Once in a while my mother would bring home a copy of American *Vogue*. This was a good enough reason for me to throw a party for all the schoolgirls. We would sit on the floor with the magazine and dream about wearing the clothes. I taught myself how to sketch the designs and make patterns. By the time I left Leningrad I was making clothes, sewing foreign labels on them, and selling them on the black market."

Having lived in New York City for four years now, Eugenia is more realistic. "And I'm not just a dress designer, y'know. I also do jewelry and soon I hope to be designing furniture. Any good designer should be able to design anything."

Eugenia, Bayard, Michael Wylde, and Chryst outside Modern Girls.

Out-of-towners probably wouldn't know that saying "Soho" to a cabbie will get them there. Soho is short for "south of Houston Street," the Mason-Dixon line that separates the former artists' district from Greenwich Village.

Let's call it "New Soho." As in platinum hair and platinum American Express cards, New Soho. "I saw Pat Boone shoes at Mary Boone gallery" in New Soho. Dean & Deluca Beluga caviar, New Soho. Diane B. and Agnes B. are in New Soho. Keith Haring's funhouse gallery, New Soho. Rizzoli books and Turpan Sanders, too, on West Broadway in New Soho. Few artists in residence (A.I.R.) still live and work in New Soho.

Some, like neo-expressionist painter Jean Michel Basquiat, live and work on the strip that realtors refer to as "Noho"—north of Houston but east of Broadway to the Bowery, the boulevard that borders the East Village. Locals, who have to step over transients from the men's shelter on the Bowery and overeager window washers on Broadway, also call this area "Boho."

Art and Commerce. Fashion and Realty. Or is it Reality?

Jeannie: "Isn't it great? It's Romeo's. He doesn't even know I'm wearing it."

OHOBOHO

"It's so gloomy out," sighs Jeannie, as she steps out onto Prince Street for a breath of fresh air. "It's a great day to stay in bed." She stretches her arms out in a yawn. "I guess that's why I'm wearing this smoking jacket, 'cause I'd rather be indoors than out here." She pulls the satin collar tight around her neck, then turns around to model her marvelous red velvet coat. "Isn't it great?" she says, as if it were sable. "It's Romeo's," she whispers, just in case he's within earshot. "He doesn't even know I'm wearing it."

"I don't know if I can sign this," Terry says, when asked to sign a model's release on the corner of Bond and Broadway. Her multicolored Mondrian jacket catches our eye. "Just about everything I'm wearing I've collected around the world," says Terry, a high-fashion model originally from South Africa. "This is, actually, a skiing jacket that I picked up in Florence," she says, fingering the lapel. "My dress is by Norma Kamali, and I got this belt in London. Oh, and these stockings came from a fashion show."

Terry: "Just about everything I'm wearing I've collected around the world."

"No, this isn't a *real* mole," says Charlene Gatz, pointing out the beauty mark above her mouth. She is on Thompson Street, walking back to Girl Loves Boy hair salon after running an errand. "I did it with an eye pencil. I think moles are sexy, especially on blondes."

The white skull tattooed on her left arm isn't real either. "Axel did this with body paint," she says. "He's into *skull*pture—silver and gold jewelry of bear claws and eagle claws, monkey skulls and bat skulls—really wild stuff!" Charlene exclaims.

She is wearing a strip of black lace as a headband. Her pale-white makeup, hot-pink lipstick, and platinum-blond hair make her look more like a Hell's Angels' angel. On her wrists is an assortment of baubles—ball chains from a hardware store on Canal Street, countless black rubber bracelets, and an expensive Seiko tank watch.

"I've had this watch for a long time," says Charlene. "I don't know why they call it a tank watch. Maybe it's for underwater sports, like skin-diving."

SOHO

Charlene: "Axel did this with body paint. He's into *skull*pture."

Charlotte out to lunch in Comme des Garçons's great standing King Tut hat.

"I'm just going over to Food [a restaurant] to pick up something for lunch," says Charlotte, dressed as if she's going to a nun's ball on a Saturday afternoon. Heads turn as she strides past a few puzzled out-of-downtowners.

"My clothes are by Comme des Garçons, right here on Wooster Street," she says. "So are my hat and gloves." Charlotte spreads her arms out to show off her "wings." "Like my gloves?" she asks. "It's all one piece; the two hands are connected by a strip of material that's almost a yard long."

More show and tell. "I got these shoes last year at Parachute," Charlotte continues. "They're by Freestyle. I wear them all the time 'cause they're so comfortable. With dresses, pants, out dancing, anything. They're men's shoes, only for women. You know what I mean."

Patsy: "These Walker's work real well with these Gaultier socks."

"These were a gift from a friend," says Patsy Abbott, clicking the heels of her brocade shoes on West Broadway. "They're from Walker's of London, and they work real well with all my clothes. They look real good with this pair of Gaultier socks, too.

"And they're a lot of fun." She smiles. "My friend was right on target. They're unlike any shoes I've ever seen in America."

51

"I like clothes that are free and easy because I'm a free-spirited kind of person." Julinda Singleton brings what looks like a hip heavy chain necklace up over her head, threads it through her yellow Yamaha moped, then secures it around a pole.

"I look for clothes that say 'Julinda.'" About her khaki-and-black outfit, she says, "I bought this at Diane B. on West Broadway. It's by Castelbejac, and I call it my 'thing.'" She has a mischievous look on her face that suddenly changes when she says, "Some clothes you have to pay a lot of money for. But I pay it only if I can get a lot of use out of it. Like, I can actually wear this ten to fifteen different ways. I can wear the black half or the khaki half—as a dress, skirt, or pants, with one leg in, one leg out, arms tied around the waist. . . .

"It all depends on how I'm feeling at the time," she says, "and I'm obviously in a very fun, playful kind of mood today 'cause I also have on this hat!" On top of her head is a black wool jersey fez by Comme des Garçons, knotted in the middle like a French pastry. "It's shaped like an ice cream cone, and it should hang down like a jester's hat. But I twisted it in a knot, I guess, because I'm in knots a lot."

"Great Jones Cafe is my favorite place to have breakfast on Sunday morning," says Gary Gerard Robinson as he waits outside for his friend Rags to show up. "Afternoon, mostly. Depends on what time I get in at night." He talks about his clothes. "Right now I'm wearing my favorite shoes from London. They're handmade and hand-embroidered with real gold thread. I got them at New Republic, right next to the Canal Street Flea Market. I have a pair in maroon, too, and green ones on order. They're real comfortable." He lights a cigarette. "I bought this jacket at the Berkeley Flea Market years ago, when I used to live there. My pants are by Koos in Soho, and the scarf is Guatemalan. A friend's mother gave me this antique rhinestone brooch by Eisenberg. And my necklace is by Robert Lee Morris, from Artwear on West Broadway."

Gary obviously knows what he's talking about. "I'm associate fashion director of Interview magazine," he mentions, "as well as a freelance stylist and art director. During the day I wear my own version of the Brooks Brothers look, for when I have to go to designer showrooms and borrow clothes for a shooting." He then adds, "I want to look like I can take care of the clothes, y'know.

"Basically," he says, "I dress according to my mood. It doesn't take me long to get dressed. I just pick up what's ironed and throw it on." He shrugs. "If I'm going where it doesn't matter whether my clothes are pressed or not, I wear it like it is."

Julinda: "I can actually wear this 'thing' ten to fifteen different ways."

Gary: "I just pick up what's ironed and throw it on."

Andy: "The country look is very cultural, so it speaks to everyone."

Naoko: "My mother sent me these pants from Comme des Garcons in Japan."

"I'm a typical city boy," says Andy Tse, wearing a Jean Paul Gaultier country cardigan and a black-and-white checked poncho by Castelbejac. Andy is originally from Hong Kong. "I can't possibly see myself living in the country, but as far as dress goes, I like it. I guess that's why I bought these boots in Paris. They're Norwegian work boots from the countryside, and they're very warm.

"The country look is very cultural, so it speaks to everyone," he explains. "Because it's never really 'in,' it never goes out of style. Like this!" He swirls his coat as if it were a bullfighter's cape. "This is nothing but a country blanket coat that I've had for a couple of years. "I see myself in a rocking chair, wearing this coat when I'm seventy," he says, wistfully. "Maybe by then I'll be living in the country."

"My mother sent me these pants from Comme des Garçons in Japan," Naoko Hirose says in her soft, chic Japanese accent. She's describing her black-noir wardrobe. A student from Ifu, a small town in Japan, her English is still new but her personal style is très nouveau.

She goes on. "My leggings are by Norma Kamali, and the rest is antique." She's wearing black kung fu shoes, with no socks. "I bought these shoes for only three dollars at a market on the street," Naoko explains. "On Forty-second Street where I take the train to New Jersey."

Naoko wears black lipstick by Mary Quant, topped with a silver shade. "I mix lots of blue and purple shadows on my eyelids," she says. "I wear regular foundation during the day, but at night," she pauses, "I go all white, like Kabuki. I use white powder from China, the one in a small, square, flowered box. I think you can get it at Patricia Field. They have the best makeup."

53

A Yellow taxicab pulls up on Thompson Street in Soho and two big heads of hair step out. It's Lara in warlocks, Girl Loves Boy's recent British import, and Tommy Gunn in a black fishnet body stocking and leather metal-stud regalia. Romeo daSilva, the salon's co-owner, nods good morning from the bench out front where he's drinking his first cappuccino. His black nylon dreadlocks swing from his beret as he welcomes Lara's next "victim." Only eighteen and a graduate of Antenna, King's Road's rave hair salon, Lara is bringing long hair back to the eighties. Her specialty is hair extensions, long pieces of fake hair that are woven into the hair, then teased, braided, or dreaded for the "big hair" look.

Down the street the Tan twins are walking up, both smiling and ready for new haircuts. In identical China

Rasta avant-garde: Tommy, Lara, and Angel outside Girl Loves Boy.

R A S T

bobs, it's hard to tell Jessica from Geraldine. Romeo grins because he can't tell them apart either.

Yuséff arrives, the only real Rasta dreadhead in the salon, which makes sense—he's black, with a finely chiseled face that suggests American Indian. He likes the nouveau tribal look and ties spiderwebbed shreds of Betsey Johnson rags and yellow nylon extensions into his hair, sometimes even bleaching a dread red or dying it aqua. He drops a cassette of Prince's *Purple Rain* into the tape deck and the workday begins.

Sunday is *not* a day of rest at Girl Loves Boy.

On her day off from behind the counter at Patricia Field and a week before her wedding, Yuko arrives with her sister, who's visiting from San Francisco. Yuséff will be styling her bridal-do, a

Lara and Charlene work on Tommy's hair: candle wax, toupee gum, and Monofibre nylon.

A V A N T

Blade Runner platinum-blond geisha vision. He disappears into the back room, reappears with a bowlful of lavender cakemix-looking stuff which he stirs with a brush, then applies to Yuko's hair in sections. This is Step One of what he calls a double-process bleach job: "Oriental hair is black-black and most resistant to bleach, so I have to apply it to the hair twice. I use a low-volume peroxide so it's milder to the scalp, to avoid any burns. Then after the second application I condition the hair with an oil treatment to make it feel like hair again, to put back some of the oil that's stripped from the hair in the process. This way it won't have that feeling of dry straw, that burnt-out look." Bob Marley's "Rastaman Vibration" is playing now, and Yuséff does this little dance around Yuko's head to the music.

Debbie leaves the phones to run off to Frusen Glädjé for ice cream. Tommy wants her to pick up a ham-and-cheese sandwich on the way, please. He's waiting for Lara to add more extensions to his head. Nights when he's not performing as backup singer of Grandmaster Melle Mel & the Furious Five, you can find Tommy Gunn at the door of Pizza-A-Go-Go, entertaining as nightclub host.

It took Tommy an hour to get dressed this morning and only ten minutes to do his makeup. He wears makeup every day, sometimes more, some days less. Some nights he even sleeps with his makeup on, but he doesn't advise it. "All the beauty books say, 'Don't sleep with your makeup on, remove it.'"

He describes his daytime look: "I like to use pancake a lot. I think it's fun. You can have a hangover from the night before and you throw pancake on and you come out looking fresh. It covers everything! I mean, *everything*! Then I use powder after that, then lots of black eyeliner. I *love*

eyeliner! And what I'm using right now is silver lipstick. I like light colors for that beach effect, either that or yellow. It depends on what I'm wearing. I like my lips really pale, almost pale yellowish-white. For a male, red lipstick doesn't make it. And I use mascara."

He folds his hands to show off his nails. He's painted them white, matte white. What color is his own hair? "Gosh, I forgot. I think it was dark brown." Tommy grew up in Manhattan's Chinatown. His father is Cantonese and his mother is Puerto Rican. "You see, blonds have more fun. That's why I did it." To prove his point, he squints like a tiger and growls.

Lara walks over with a handful of

hair in her hand. Charlene assists, armed with a lit white candle and what looks like a bottle of glue. "First, I weave the fake hair into Tommy's hair, then I add the toupee gum," Lara explains in her London drawl. "I don't use glue. This is spirit gum, actually, and it rinses out after a couple of washes and doesn't damage the hair."

Tommy sits patiently in front of the mirror as the girls stand over his head like two alchemists contemplating a transformation. "I cover his real hair by twisting the fake hair around it, then fuse it together with candle wax. This way his own hair never touches the flame."

With a whole head of extensions down to his waist, Tommy has his hair teased up front into a bouffant. Lara zaps it with a can of hair spray. "These fake hair

Debbie's teen-angel outfit: white leather miniskirt, tight sweater, and ID anklet.

Tommy's makeup tip: "I like light colors for that beach effect."

"I cover his real hair by twistin' the fake hair around," says Lar "then fuse it together with candle wax. This way his own hair never touches the flame."

extensions are made out of nylon by an English company called Monofibre," says Lara. "You can wash it with shampoo or Woolite. You don't need a cream rinse. We [Girl Loves Boy] carry it in about fifteen to twenty colors, including day-glo orange and green, and the natural colors as well. I've had mine in for about seven months, but I recommend redoing them after three or four months because your own hair grows out and it becomes matted." Lara charges $200 for an entire head of extensions, $120 for half a head, and $30 apiece for a braid, dreadlock, or a ragtail.

In the next chair, Romeo spins Jessica around and hands her a

mirror so she can take a look at the back of her head. The first cut is finished.

"This is my variation of Vidal Sassoon's sixties Peggy Moffatt cut," he says. "I took the whole back off by shingling it up real high. Shingling is very hot now." Geraldine nods in approval of her sister's new "do."

"I buzzed the hair right off of a big comb with an electric trimmer. Basically, this is a barber's technique. I always use a big comb and big scissors, especially for blunt cuts. It gives it more flair, more style, and it makes it easier to chop off a whole bunch of hair at one time." This approach is totally opposite from the Sassoon school of haircutting, where Romeo learned to cut hair in small sections, using a little scissors and a little comb.

Romeo still hasn't taken off his wool beret or plaid jacket. "With both of them having hair all one length to the shoulder, it's not only hard to tell them apart, it's boring. I'm going to give Geraldine an asymmetrical cut by taking one side high above the ear and shaping it into an angle all around the back. It will look lopsided, and the longer side will come down in front to a bob length at the chin. Then, on the shorter side, I'll layer and feather it where she parts her hair so that when the front is brushed forward and to the side, it won't look like a typical Oriental blunt haircut."

He pulls a crimping iron out of the closet and plugs it in. While

The Tan twins, Geraldine and Jessica, in matching Espada dresses: not your typical China bob haircuts.

"For her makeup", says Yuséff, "I figure on going very soft and simple, as a contrast to the bizarreness of her hair that's buzzed on the sides, bleached out, and blue."

Yuséff gives Yuko a "chemical cut."

waiting for it to heat up, Romeo mists her hair with water. "This is an easy way to add body to your hair and give it a different texture." He takes a small section of hair and clamps it between the hot tongs, using both hands. Two minutes later Geraldine's sleek black hair is waffled.

Now Yuséff cuts Yuko's hair, and his hands fly over her head. You can hardly see the small razor as shards of platinum hair float to the floor. "I use a razor to get a slithery effect . . . and thinning shears. But I don't have to cut very much because the bleaching did a lot of my work for me. When you go pale white you're gonna lose a certain amount of fullness . . . the hair thins out a bit. So I gave her what I call a 'chemical cut.'" Yuséff smiles, obviously pleased with his witticism. On the right side of her head he ties in a lavender fake-hair extension, and on top, a baby-blue ponytail. He starts applying a very pale liquid foundation to Yuko's forehead. "For her makeup I figure on going very soft and

simple, as a contrast to the bizarreness of her hair that's buzzed on the sides, bleached out, and blue." He puts liquid eyeliner on her eyes, yellow eye shadow from Patricia Field, then accents her eyebrows a little.

"Sometimes you can get into a very heavy punk look that some people don't necessarily see as beauty," says Yuséff. "Basically, my work is fantasy—that's my stand. I want people to react favorably to it and not find it repulsive to look at." He paints Yuko's lips red. "I've outgrown the shock of it all. I don't like shock treatment. I find it boring. I think it scares away more people than anything else. There are certain elements that will be shocking, of course, but there should also be another element that's alluring to the point where you say, 'My God, this is fantastic!'"

Girl Loves Boy sells many hair-care items over the counter. Some are imported by Girl Loves Boy; others are sold at retail counters throughout the country. Adriana Barrett, co-owner of the salon, recommends these gels, mousses, and sprays:

Blue Spirit High Energy Gel ($12). "This is from Antenna hair salon in London," says Adriana. "It comes in a jar [similar to Dippity-do, only blue] and it makes your hair stand up thick and firm."

Petro White ($6). "Also an Antenna product, this hair grease will slick your hair back like the old-fashioned Brilliantine."

Mousse de Créme Soft 'n Light Styling Foam ($6). "Good for blonds and people with fine hair. This mousse gives the hair a lighter, more natural feeling . . . good for uptown types. It does the job but doesn't leave hair with a sticky or stiff feeling."

Peter Hartz Pro-structure Styling Glaze ($7). "A little lighter than Aveda gel, which is better for thick, coarse hair. Good for curly hair—that wet look—but if you want your hair to stand up stiff, follow this with a good hair spray."

Aero lak Hair Lacquer ($3). "This is the strongest hair spray around. Perfect for that finishing touch."

Fizz-in Colour Shampoo-out Haircolour ($14). "This is a temporary hair color rinse for people with light-color hair. It also makes the hair stiffer while it puts in a hint of color. Comes in all artificial shades."

Framesi Color-Enhanced Styling Gel ($8). "Like Fizz-in, but with more color. A lot of people with black hair use this for blue highlights."

Belson's Crimper Iron ($25). "I like this brand of crimper best because of its streamlined design. It's easier to hold, and the crimp stays in your hair all day long. If it's damp out, comb a light setting gel through your hair, then use the iron."

Girl loves boy, boy loves girl: Romeo with Jeannie, wearing a silk-screen sweatshirt.

RARE HAIR

eon is with Kaetti at Pizza-A-Go-Go. His hair is white-white, and it shines like ice at high noon. So how does he get his hair to do that?

"This is paint. Oil paint," says Leon. He offers you his head to feel. Sure enough. Paint. "You can't get this kind of white from bleach. I take very good care of my hair. Also, I'm not into this blue-hair crap like a lot of these kids. Before, I used to paint it black." Leon doesn't say how he gets the paint out of his hair, assuming he ever wants to.

A few weeks later, Leon and Kaetti are at another club, Danceteria. Kaetti's long, yellow blond hair is now a perfect match for Leon's very short, ultrawhite hair. It's Kaetti who almost reveals the secret.

"I use a chemical," she says, referring to the cleaning agent for her hair. What chemical? "I'd rather

not say," she goes on. "But it takes two hours."

Whereas Leon sticks to oil paint, Kaetti is a little less adventurous. "No, this is acrylic," she says, rubbing her bristly hair. Kaetti does, however, use oil and acrylic paint on her legs. How does that work?

"I lubricate them with an oil first," she says.

Back at Pizza-A-Go-Go, Donna the bartender sports a *Road Warrior* T-shirt to go with her road-warrior hair. "I use soap and hair spray," says Donna, taking a break from behind the bar. "I lather it up. It dries. I spray it with hair spray, and then the hair separates." Instant dreads.

A more radical rasta look is achieved through hair extensions. "Lara at Girl Loves Boy did my extensions," says Molly, who works at the Patricia Field boutique. Molly's hair extensions aren't

Oil paint gives Leon's hair that ultrawhite look.

dreads; they shoot up freestyle through a scarf she's wrapped around her head. "Instead of going to get my hair cut," says Molly, "I get it lengthened. Lasts about three months. This has been in for five months, and it's real Barbie Doll. I'm having it done again soon."

Outside Patricia Field, designers Maria and Charles Minichiello, whose clothes appear inside, have this to say about their heads: "It's called a 'plait,'" says Charles, tugging at the long, braided strand of hair that runs out of his military beret and along the collar of his leather jacket. "I just care for it like it was my baby. My girl's going to wear it on her belt when I lop it off. A conquest!"

Maria has no such intentions for her own hair. "My hair's crimped," says Maria, explaining how it stands up off her head. "I put in a little Dippity-do and leave it wet— I don't have the time to let it dry—

and then I put on hair spray."

In the East Village, Sur Rodney (Sur) is sitting outside the art gallery Gracie Mansion on Avenue A. His head bears all kinds of geometric patterns, but when someone points out that his haircut resembles the stars-and-stripes of the American flag, Sur Rodney begs to disagree.

"It's supposed to look like Gracie's office," he says, referring to his partner in art and business, Gracie Mansion.

Two artists, Dennis and Cornelia, cut and shaved his hair. "One did one side and one did the other. I don't remember which."

Rodney wasn't turned off by the experience. In fact, he recommends it. "Usually artists are the best [haircutters]. They go, 'Hey, your hair looks great. I have this idea.'"

Besides a great haircut, Rodney also has a great ascot. "It's a rag. I

Fake hair: Molly has blond hair extensions while Melody wears a "cheap black wig from London."

Donna has a *Road Warrior* T-shirt to go with her road-warrior hair. "I use soap and hair spray. I lather it up. It dries. I spray it with hair spray, and then the hair separates."

Donna with instant dreads.

found it in the trash on Avenue C."

Over on St. Mark's, a woman has her hair extensions pinned up into something Joan Crawford would have scrubbed a million linoleum floors for. "You think so?" asks the woman, who's just bought some coffee-to-go at Café Orlin on St. Mark's. She lives around here. East Villagers get their coffee and cappuccino at Café Orlin. Most of the cafés farther west are for the tourists. The woman is in a hurry

and can't be photographed, but "will be back this way" in about half an hour.

Fifteen minutes later, she's back. "You know," she says, "I think it's more like Betty Rubble in 'The Flintstones.' " What? "My hair!"

She poses, then takes a few minutes to read the model's release form before signing. "No, I want this taken out," she says, pointing to the line about using a "fictitious name" with her photo.

"My hair's crimped," says Maria, explaining how it stands up off her head. "I put in a little Dippity-do, and leave it wet. Then I put on hair spray."

Charles and Maria: the long and the short of it.

Fine. She crosses the line out, then signs her name: "Vaudevillia."

A few minutes later, a young man and woman stroll by the café. His bright yellow hair is a perfect match for his bright yellow jacket. So how does he get his hair to stay in spikes?

"Is there money in this for me?" he asks. Handed a fiver, the man—whose name is Mike—excitedly takes off his yellow jacket to be photographed, but is urged to put it back on. The jacket has lots of gold braids, and it looks spectacular.

"It's hers," says Mike, pointing to his companion.

"It's a band jacket," says the girl, who calls herself "Machete Eddy." She thinks Mike should have asked for more money. They pose together. Then Mike does it alone. So about those spikes in his hair . . .

"Unflavored gelatin," says Mike,

Vaudevillia in a "Flintstone" hairdo.

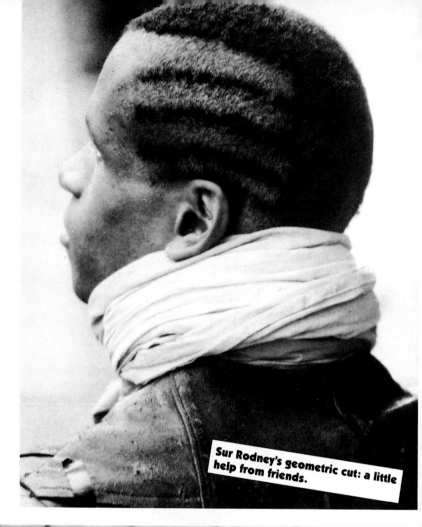

Sur Rodney's geometric cut: a little help from friends.

talking about how they're molded. The powdered gelatin is mixed with water and applied directly to his wet hair.

"Knox," adds Machete, giving the brand name to use.

"Put it in a bowl in the fridge first," says Mike.

"Yeah," adds Machete, "it's best if the Knox is cold."

And the yellow color of his hair?

"After I bleach it, my hair's like this naturally. It's been bleached so much, y'know, I don't really need the Knox anymore."

That afternoon, walking the streets, Mike has his spikes in place, but the yellow hair is now streaked green. Later, Machete Eddy has the same green color in her hair. It's definitely worth a shot.

"Get any more stoogies yet?" asks Machete, passing by. This time she's not stopping.

Julinda's pillbox Afro: "I like it easy and simple. One time I ev shaved my head."

64

"Unflavored gelatin," says Mike, talking about how his spikes are molded. "Knox," adds Machete Eddy. "Put it in a bowl in the fridge first," says Mike. "It's best if the Knox is cold," says Machete.

Mike's spikes no longer need the Knox.

Postscript: Vaudevillia is buying clothes at Patricia Field. A couple of weeks have passed since she was spotted on St. Mark's. Her hair is still blond and curly in front. But what's happened to the rest of it—those splendid mounds of pinned-up hair? Somebody practically shaved the back of her head!

"You know, I wanted to tell you something," Vaudevillia begins right off. "My hair didn't look like Betty Rubble of 'The Flintstones.' It's *Wilma* Flintstone!"

But what happened to her hair?

"They took out the hair extensions."

Obviously. But why?

Vaudevillia ponders a moment, then reveals the only inarguable justification for changing one's fashion.

"Oh, I just got tired of it."

Jackie and Marc at Danceteria: blue dye and a shave for her, Knox and hair spray for him.

"Angel wings": Ti Ti and Juan at De Martino's.

"I spray each strand with Aero lak before I go on to the next strand," explains Ti Ti. "With a comb and my hands, I then shape the hair into two wings."

NITE ONLY

Nightclub doormen downtown may not know her name, but they know her look. Make that *looks*. "Generally, I'm smaller than everybody else," says Ti Ti Chimente, who is ultra-petite, "but they see me."

While others wait in line, the ropes part for Ti Ti. Definitely, the clubs need her and her looks. All Ti Ti needs is her imagination . . . and a few aerosol cans.

"I love to look extravagant," says Ti Ti, a makeup artist and hairstylist. "But you don't have to be wild all the time. Just when you want to be."

That statement would come as a gentle shock to the people who know Ti Ti through her work at the Michael Gottfried Studio. After all, her hair color, hairstyle, and makeup have been known to

"Beyond death": a Woolworth wig worn backward.

"Cat": Streaks 'n Tips and a can of Aero lak.

change by the hour.

"That's just the point," explains Ti Ti . Her gentle, Spanish-accented voice rarely rises above a whisper. "If you have your hair dyed neon-blue or cut in a Mohawk, you're stuck with it. Myself, I prefer a variety of different looks, and so I keep my hair simple and longish. That way you have more to play with."

After a very late night/early morning of dancing at Area, Ti Ti hunts for fish at De Martino's on Eighth Avenue with her friend, designer Juan Pisonero. Her makeup and "angel wing" hair match the bold geometric design of her coat ("No, it's not leather; it's cheap vinyl") and dress, which was designed by Juan. At the moment, Juan is getting inspiration among the red snappers for another creation: food or fashion,

only he knows.

Ti Ti achieves her different looks—all of which she has names for—with flashy geometric makeup designs, and hairstyles and coloring that are strictly one-nite-only. This is instant beauty that washes off and out.

Instead of cutting her hair into an exotic shape, Ti Ti gives herself "angel wings" by teasing the hair. "I tease one strand at a time," Ti Ti explains at the Blue Plate, a fast-food eatery up the avenue from De Martino's. "I spray each strand with Aero lak [a hair spray] before I go on to the next strand. With a comb and my hands, I then shape the hair into two wings."

How much hair spray does it take to keep two wings in orbit? "Oh, about a quarter of a can," Ti Ti estimates, not quite sure she's used enough on her own hair.

"Then I spray one wing with Orange Glo, the other with Blue Glo." This temporary hair coloring is sold under the commercial name of Streaks 'n Tips, which is produced by Nestlés.

The color is not permanent; it comes off with a good shampooing. However, there are risks. "If your hair is bleached, I don't recommend that you use it," says Ti Ti. "Some of the color might stay in the hair. Also, since the coloring is water-soluble, it's best not to use it on a rainy night unless you carry a very large umbrella."

Ti Ti uses a slightly different approach to achieve the "cat" look. Model Janet Murtha, unlike Ti Ti, has very curly, kinky hair, which can be a problem when it comes to shaping. For this reason, Ti Ti sprays on a conditioner, Infusium 23, which takes away the frizzies.

Ti Ti blow-dries the hair and then teases it, smoothing it with a comb. Hair spray and color spray (Streaks 'n Tips's Red Glo) prevent the hair from losing its shape, which in this case is something like a well-cared-for sphinx.

For those who worry about teasing-induced split ends, Ti Ti recommends another method for keeping wild-style hair in place. "First, your hair must be dry. Then with a dryer, blow the hair into position. While the hot air is blowing, spray the hair with Aero lak." This procedure has been known to require three or more hands. "The combination of the hot air and the spray keeps your hair in place without teasing the hair and risking split ends. This is a secret tip. Very few people know about it," insists Ti Ti, who is not prone to exaggeration—despite her appearance.

Split ends are no problem in creating Ti Ti's "beyond death" look. Here, the hair is synthetic. "I got the wig at Woolworth's," says Ti Ti, who counts the store as one of her absolute favorites. Ti Ti teases and sprays the synthetic hair. The wig can be worn the way it was designed, in a bob with bangs in front. "But I prefer to have it worn backwards," says Ti Ti, "with the back in front. It makes the hair appear bigger."

Bigger?

"Yes, you know, 'big hair.' Longer and layered and wild." The wig is from the Goldentex Collection and costs about $20.

For her "future antique" look, Ti Ti doesn't tease the hair or use hair spray to keep it looking big. "Sugar is the key," she says. "Mix half an ounce of sugar with three ounces of water and apply it to your already-wet hair with a spray bottle. Then braid the wet hair, tying the ends with rubber bands or ribbons to keep them tight and in place. When the hair dries and you undo the ribbons, the hair looks crimped.

"It's safer than using a crimping iron," advises Ti Ti. "Many unprofessionals burn their hair that way." She also recommends that you not brush or comb sugared hair. It will take away that "big hair" effect. "But you might want to tease it just a little."

Ti Ti, who buys most of her wardrobe in thrift shops and flea markets, got her gray satin gown in London a few years ago. "It's Ann-Margret's dress from *Tommy*," she explains. "I just had to take it in a little at the top."

But who's looking at the dress?

"Big hair" is not difficult to create. Ti Ti's makeup is another matter. The illustration here is for her "aquamarine" face. Ti Ti suggests the following nine steps to recreate this particular look:

1. Over a very pale liquid foundation, apply a translucent blue powder to the entire face.

2. Dust the eyelids with lavender powder eye shadow.

3. From the crease of the eyelid to the eyebrow, apply pale-green powder eye shadow. This color should extend outside the eyelids and sweep up toward the temples.

4. Small dots of blue and green eye cream may be applied over the green shadow for added highlights.

5. Under the green shadow, apply shades of lavender, blue, and pale-green eye shadows as seen in the illustration.

6. Line each eyelid with a dark-blue eyeliner, and from the corner of the eye, following the direction of the shadow placed earlier, extend the liner in a squiggly line.

7. With a blue pencil, draw in a wavy eyebrow as above.

8. Outline lips with a dark-blue pencil.

9. Apply lavender lipstick.

Aquamarine

Neo-Tribal

Holocaust

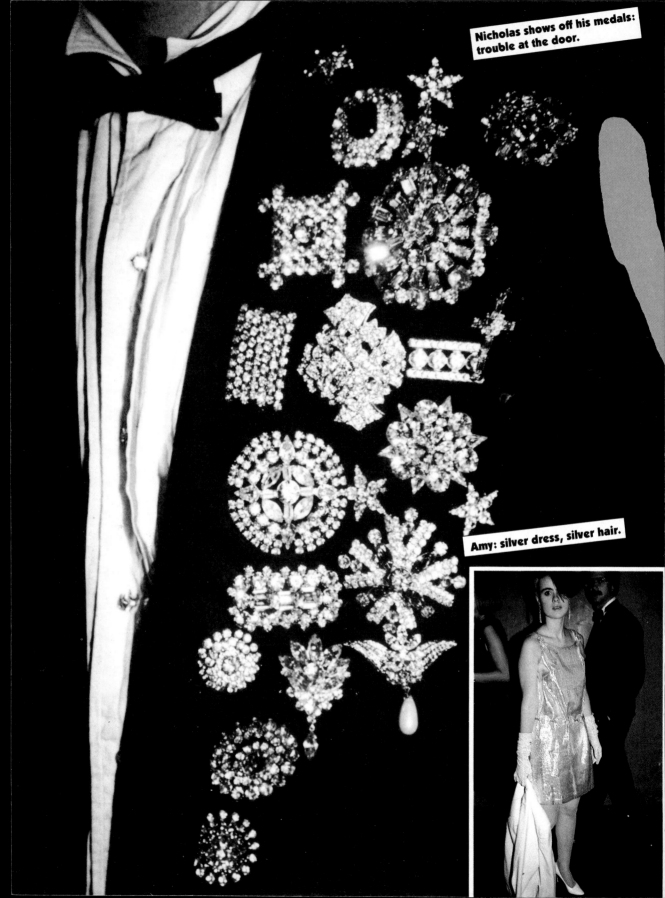

Nicholas shows off his medals: trouble at the door.

Amy: silver dress, silver hair.

Wild Style

"We're the Fashion Nazis," says Joe Brese, the main doorman at Area, Manhattan's hottest nightclub. Joe decides who gets to enter the club, and more important, who does not. "You can't let everyone in. And so we have to judge people on fashion, on what they're wearing."

And what they're wearing makes all the difference at Area. Part gallery, part discotheque, part three-ring circus, the club comes off like a wax museum, only here the people are alive.

It's a cold winter night. A line of limousines and taxis form on Hudson and Laight streets in Tribeca. A crowd ten deep is huddled in front of No. 157 as a bitter wind whips off the Hudson River.

"Okay!" Joe shouts above the impatient masses. "All the women in black with pearls get in!" A creature with black lipstick, black nail polish, but no pearls cuts in with the Chanel types. Joe holds back the black pair of lips. Because he has tired of her "bondage look," she's not getting past the ropes.

What makes it at the door of Area depends on Joe. At the moment he's into hats. "Men with hats get in much quicker," he says. Skirts on men can also impress. "We get three or four a night." For women, rags in the hair is a definite plus. "That Farrah Fawcett look is not." Long hair on men, though, is becoming more fashionable, Joe notices. "It goes with the oversized look in clothing," he says, quick to distinguish this new long hair from the old hippie-type cuts, which were unkempt. "It's long hair with a tidy eighties flair."

What makes a body truly memorable? Only one thing is for sure—it's more than just the body. "The way the clothes move as you watch the people walking down

the street is important," he says. Sometimes merely looking wild won't do; other times it gets you through the door. "Like the woman whose hair changes colors every night. Red. Blue. White. She always covers what has to be covered on

David Leigh suits up in his fashion-magazine jacket.

her body," Joe says, "but it's the w she exposes the skin she exposes."

Even in a world where appearances mean everything, Joe's job is not all fun. He taps his beret, a Joe Brese trademark. "Besides keeping your head

74

warm," he says about his cap, "you can hit people with them." Joe's not joking. "I've stopped going out to clubs. People come up to me and say, 'Why did you

make me wait two minutes last night?'" Joe whines, imitating too many distraught, angry customers. "I've had guys pull knives on me. So now I use a bodyguard, besides the beret. The bodyguard is written in my contract."

Obviously, violence won't get you in the door at Area. But beauty's not enough, either.

Here's what is:

"I got the dress for a dollar at a

garage sale," says Amy, who is wearing a metallic party dress à la Sandra Dee. The dress is a perfect match for the right side of her hairdo. It, too, is very silver, and about six inches shorter than the hair on the opposite side of her head. "My friend Charles cuts my hair. He's not a professional. I use Streaks 'n Tips on the side to make it silvery. Do you want to meet Charles?"

David Leigh is suited in a jacket he made from fashion magazine covers. "I just use good ol' Elmer's Glue," he says, giving away the secret of the garment's construction. "I painted on it with acrylic. Industrial diamond dust gives it that glitzy quality. They use it in New York City sidewalks, too."

"They help in getting through the door at clubs," says Nicholas, his jacket lapel littered with rhinestone medals and pins. These baubles are as practical as they are decorative, but there are problems. "Boy, it was tough getting in tonight," Nicholas admits, frustrated at his long wait outside Area. "I had to hold up my lapel so the doorman would see." Where does he buy his honors? "I pick 'em up for a dollar in antique

75

stores. Even in New York City, people gawk. 'Liberace!' they cry. Believe me, the city's not as liberal as you think."

Reno has on a terry-cloth beach jacket. He wears it like a tux. "I bought it in Ohio, of course!" he announces, almost defiant. "They have all the best thrift shops in Ohio. I make a shopping trip there at least once a year."

Andrea Bourgoise takes on Area in a skimpy rubber outfit that may have seen a former life on the underside of a Mack truck. "Brian Damage designed it," says Andréa. "It's one of a kind." Her bra has Firestone treads. So do her Spartacus arm guards. Is it hot under those tires? "No, it's a G string." Her companion Shawn has no comment.

"Oh, yes, it's real leopard," says Joe, who's wearing a real leopard chapeau and a real leopard stole and clutching a real leopard muff. He stands in front of Stephen Sprouse's futuristic window

Shawn and Andrea (right) in black rubber: "Brian Damage designed it."

Stephen and Emilio mix antique jackets, Jean Paul Gaultier, and ski pants.

display. Inside, a model in wraparound Ray-Bans and a silver jumpsuit lounges by a video monitor. "This hat belonged to my grandmother," Joe reveals.

For Bryan and Charles, it began with kilts over pants. Then came

sarongs. "I was in India," says Bryan, "and the men wear sarongs there. I'm not a great sewer, so I made one." Since it's easy, he explains how it's done: "Take fabric, put it around your waist, and crisscross it, folding it over at

the top. That keeps it in place." Bryan wears his with a belt, but says it's not necessary.

"When I go out to clubs I like to be eclectic," says Stephen. True to his word, he's wearing a tux from the fifties. The jewelry is all

secondhand thrift-store stuff. But the silk shirt, by Katherine Hamnett, and the pants, by Jean Paul Gaultier, are 1984. "I mix designers. And I put together things that cost $200 with things that cost $2."

So does Emilio, who's standing nearby. Who else in Area is wearing a red antique smoking jacket with tight acrylic ski pants?

"I dance at the Cat Club on Saturdays," says David as he takes off his cadet hat to spin on one hand. The numbers on his pants blur as he jackknifes, pops, moonwalks, then leaps in the air like Mr. MXPLTK from the Superman comics. "I get paid to dance there, but I teach break dancing, too." He makes a hieroglyphic gesture. A small crowd gathers around, leaving him a wide circle of floor space to perform in. "I never come here on weekends. It's a totally different crowd. The music doesn't even get good until after three o'clock. I'm usually here on Thursday nights. That's when all the

people are out. Downtown people."

Leaning against one wall is graffiti artist Keith Haring. He's wearing his favorite leather jacket—a brown aviator with an oil portrait of Michael Jackson on the back. Painted under it in big letters is the artist's signature, Stefano. Stefano Castronovo. "Michael Jackson is my only hero," says Keith, who takes it all back to add, "and Andy Warhol, of course. And Jean Michel Basquiat, he's my favorite painter." Keith is brainstorming an idea for a poster of Brooke Shields by Richard Avedon. "I just did Grace Jones for *Interview* magazine. I painted her whole body for a photo by Robert Mapplethorpe. But I have to come up with something totally different for Brooke, maybe something with the theme of 'America's Sweetheart,' which she is, you know."

Joey has on a gold Sally Beers coat under his antique brocade smoking jacket. But his hat is what's really special. "It's an early seventies pimp hat," he says. "One of my thrift-store finds."

Susan Balcunas is wearing brocade, too. "This is a pajama jacket," she says. "I made it this afternoon in two hours." Even more striking is her platinum hair. "When it's dry, I put enough Dippity-do in to dampen it, and I twist it into small sections. I then

Fresh and fashion-forward: Lorraine with Naveda.

put a pin through each twist to hold the hair tight. Like pin curls, only straight up instead." Susan smiles, suddenly looking like the queen of hearts. "It dries in about two hours." Just enough time to make another jacket.

Keith Haring in Stefano aviator jacket: "Michael Jackson is my only hero. . . ."

"I have a postcard of two New Guinean warriors with platinum hair that was taken in the Solomon Islands in 1893," says Lorraine Bethel, posing next to her friend, Naveda. "I bleached my hair because I wanted to change its look without altering its natural texture. Although most people think it's punk-influenced, they make the usual mistake of thinking the imitative style is the original one." She grins, revealing a dimple on her chin. "So I see my hair and own personal style as an extension of the traditional Third World talent for drama, wit, and funky genius. My only problem is the blonde jokes, but nobody ever said that being fashion-forward or 'fresh' would be easy."

Joey and Susan: Dippity-do, brocades, and a pimp's hat.

Elizabeth reveals her secret: "White electrical tape."

Elizabeth Saltzman watches her own reflection in a window at Area. Her see-through vinyl dress with faux-fur hemline was designed by Pedro and Alejandro. White panties, garter belt, and stockings block the view. And what kind of tape does Elizabeth recommend for the nipples? "White electrical tape," she reports. Is it hot inside a vinyl dress? "Feel my chest!" exclaims Elizabeth. Sure enough, very hot. The *paparazzi* almost blind the woman with their flashbulbs. But two hours later, covering the same turf, she walks by in the dark. A photographer passes her, but doesn't even raise his camera. "Oh, yeah, I know," cries Elizabeth. "Already old hat!"

ANTIQUE BOUTIQUE
712-714 Broadway, N.Y., N.Y. 10003
AREA
157 Hudson Street, N.Y., N.Y. 10013
ARTWEAR
409 West Broadway, N.Y., N.Y. 10012
ASTOR PLACE HAIR CUTTERS
2 Astor Place, N.Y., N.Y. 10003
BEULAH LAND
162 Avenue A, N.Y., N.Y. 10009
BLACK MARKET
307 East Ninth Street, N.Y., N.Y. 10003
CAFÉ ORLIN
41 St. Mark's Place, N.Y., N.Y. 10003
COMME DES GARÇONS
116 Wooster Street, N.Y., N.Y. 10012
DANCETERIA
30 West Twenty-first Street, N.Y., N.Y. 10010
DIANE B.
426 West Broadway, N.Y., N.Y. 10012
8 BC
337 East Eighth Street, N.Y., N.Y. 10009
ENZ'S
5 St. Mark's Place, N.Y., N.Y. 10003
FOOD
127 Prince Street, N.Y., N.Y. 10012
GIRL LOVES BOY
63 Thompson Street, N.Y., N.Y. 10012
GRACIE MANSION
167 Avenue A, N.Y., N.Y. 10009
GREAT JONES CAFE
54 Great Jones Street, N.Y., N.Y. 10012
KOOS
72 Thompson Street, N.Y., N.Y. 10013
MICHAEL GOTTFRIED STUDIO
853 Seventh Avenue, N.Y., N.Y. 10019
MODERN GIRLS
169 Thompson Street, N.Y., N.Y. 10012
NEW REPUBLIC
15–17 Greene Street, N.Y., N.Y. 10013
109 ST. MARK'S PLACE
109 St. Mark's Place, N.Y., N.Y. 10009
PARACHUTE
121 Wooster Street, N.Y., N.Y. 10012
PATRICIA FIELD
10 East Eighth Street, N.Y., N.Y. 10003
THE PIT
31 St. Mark's Place, N.Y., N.Y. 10003
PIZZA-A-GO-GO
121 West Thirty-first Street, N.Y., N.Y. 10001
PYRAMID LOUNGE
101 Avenue A, N.Y., N.Y. 10009